yahweh war
& Tribal
Confederation

yahweh war
& Tribal Confederation
Reflections upon Israel's Earliest History

Rudolf Smend

*translated from the
second edition
by*
Max Gray Rogers

ABINGDON PRESS
nashville and new york

SET UP, PRINTED, AND BOUND BY THE
PARTHENON PRESS, AT NASHVILLE,
TENNESSEE, UNITED STATES OF AMERICA

Translator's Foreword

Since the last quarter of the nineteenth century, the name Rudolf Smend has been a familiar one within circles of Old Testament scholarship. The penetrating insight which the elder Smend brought to bear in the wake of the documentary hypothesis is now reflected almost a century later in the work of his grandson and namesake who is presently Professor of Old Testament at the University of Münster. In this study Professor Smend has endeavored to explore the relationship between the confederation of the twelve tribes of Israel and the phenomenon which he describes as the war of Yahweh. His investigation is both thorough and discerning; his conclusions, stimulating and suggestive of new directions. In a real sense, Professor Smend's concept of "Yahweh war" can be viewed as a kind of sequel to Professor von Rad's "Holy War."

As for the translation, I must express my gratitude to Mr. and Mrs. Franz Scheiper, to Dr. Heinrich Pfeiffer, Dr. Thomas Berberich and the Alexander von Humboldt-Stiftung, and especially to my colleague Professor John E. Steely who twice read through the manuscript and whose suggestions have been invaluable. My indebtedness to my wife for her patience and assistance far exceeds any words I could write here.

Durham, North Carolina   M.G.R.

Contents

Introduction

Israel's earliest time in Palestine has caused particular difficulties for Old Testament studies from the very beginning.
In the presentations of conservative historians certainly
enough is still being said about it. However the light which
is shed upon it there is only a faint reflection of the splendor
of the Mosaic epoch. Even Heinrich Ewald speaks about a
"serious hiatus of the times," [1] and if one moves from his
magnificent and positive presentation of Mosaic Israel, then
the continuation seems pale and drab. Even if once in awhile
"midway in the passage of these times on some exceptional
occasion a ray of indispensable light does suddenly flash
through this night," [2] it becomes even clearer that it is, as a
whole, night. How is this possible after the great beginning?
Paul Volz still asks where the work of Moses might be. He
does not find it and explains its absence by saying that
throughout history the following centuries do not maintain
the level of the great beginning.[3] This can be accepted as a
theoretical tenet of an opponent of the historical development school, the application of which, however, to Israel's
early history was already in Volz's time long since outdated.
Moses was no longer the criterion against which the Judges
were measured. For the critical historians, he was submerged
in the darkness of antiquity; what they still dared to say

[1] *Geschichte des Volkes Israel,* II (3rd ed., 1865) , 512.
[2] *Ibid.*
[3] P. Volz, *Mose und sein Werk* (2nd ed., 1932) , pp. 14-15.

9

about him was seldom positive. Thus it fell the lot of the earliest time in Canaan to be the period of origin of the Israel which is visible to us. But where was Israel then? The passages in the Book of Judges where it appears as a whole, acting and being acted upon, scholarship of the nineteenth century had dismissed to a large extent as a late framework or an unhistorical legend, and what remained was a colorful progression of sagas which had as their subject the deeds of individuals, clans or tribes, at best groups of tribes, but not of Israel as a whole. Thus there apparently was not an external organization of the nation, said Wellhausen [4] and most following him, but "a certain internal unity" which existed long "before it was expressed in a political community." Even at that time this vague statement was not wholly satisfactory, and one can understand the words with which Eduard Reuss in his *Geschichte der Heiligen Schrift Alten Testaments*[5] leaves the period of the Judges: "To the scholar of Hebraic history the figure of Samuel appears as brilliant as the rising sun in the midst of the fog of a dark, muddled antiquity." Now he comes to the ever firmer footing of sources which, indeed at first and even later still legendary, in themselves are contradictory and heterogeneous, yet which nevertheless allow an approximate presentation of the course of events, and which remarkably soon rise to the rank of genuine historiography.[6] Furthermore: from this point onward Israel is no longer only a "certain internal unity" more surmised than seen, but it can now be comprehended as a stable political entity. And this entity is now also a criterion against which the former is measured, almost the only one, once the time of Moses has been eliminated for that purpose. Thus the time of Judges appears in the first place negatively as the time "in which there was yet no king in Israel," and

---

[4] *Geschichte*, p. 28.

[5] (2nd ed., 1890), p. 145.

[6] Compare G. v. Rad, *The Problem of the Hexateuch and Other Essays* (New York: McGraw-Hill, 1966), pp. 166 ff.

positively as the preparation of the kingdom. One must assume from the beginning that therewith full justice is not done to it. However the fixed starting point is indeed quite valuable, and in this case even more so, since A. Alt in 1930 in his "The Formation of the Israelite State in Palestine" showed us this development from its institutional side and thereby called attention especially to its continuity in which the Israelite kingdom relates to certain entities of the preceding period.

However not only is our knowledge about the time in question being enriched through better information of its culmination,[7] but above all through the fact that—again in 1930—M. Noth made plausible a pre-state institution with the name Israel, namely, the sacred confederation of twelve tribes around a common central sanctuary. On the basis laid down by Noth—which Alt too had already assumed in the above mentioned work—a great deal of work has since been done, the result of which proves its capacity. Of course some have also assigned to it a weight which, as it seems to me, it cannot sustain.[8] The following investigation seeks to show this. It has to do with the relationship between the confederation of the twelve tribes of Israel and the phenomenon that G. v. Rad has described as the "Holy War in ancient Israel." In this relationship lies a problem which, in my opinion, has not yet been seen in its full trenchancy. It seems to me, namely, that in connection with the two above mentioned phenomena there is a question of a dualism which is resolved only late and then imperfectly, and that from this also certain conclusions can be drawn about the time before the conquest of the land which is no longer capable of being grasped by us today.

Throughout the following, I rely upon these two basic

---

[7] It accords with the better knowledge of its beginnings, for which we are indebted to Alt's writings about Israel's conquest of the land of Palestine.

[8] This is also the opinion of S. Herrmann, ThLZ, 87 (1962), columns 561 ff.

works of Noth and v. Rad and moreover in the last two chapters upon Noth's "Überlieferungsgeschichte des Pentateuch." My own reflections are not intended to be more than an appendix. Concerning the demonstrability of the presentation, I have no illusions. The phenomena with which one can work are for the most part of a hypothetical nature. In this area one can surmise much, but prove little. It lies in the nature of the matter and for the present cannot be changed. In view of the importance of the subject, conjectures are thus necessary if one does not wish to be satisfied with ignorance. In the following, I have nowhere aimed at a general investigation of the earliest history of Israel. I limit myself to the proposed inquiry and omit what would lead away from it.

1

Tribal Action and the Confederation of the Twelve

It is a commonplace of Old Testament scholarship that we have before us in the Song of Deborah (Judges 5) the most authentic, if not the only truly authentic, source concerning the time of the Judges. Therefore we will best begin with the question, What can be said of the Song of Deborah concerning our subject?

An Israelite coalition defeats a Canaanite coalition. Thus one might like to describe the event upon first sight. But in so doing one would do grave violence to the text and the intent of the song. In the actual portrayal of the conflict which begins in verse 19 neither Israel nor any of its tribes is any longer mentioned by name. Against the Canaanites fight the stars of Heaven (verse 20) and "the primeval brook," the Kishon (verse 21). The last crucial deed, the murder of the general Sisera, is accomplished not by Zebulun and Naphtali, much less the other tribes, but by the Kenite Jael (verses 24 ff). It is true that "the heroes" are mentioned once, not however as a special object of consideration, but as those with whom Meroz should have joined "in the aid of Yahweh" (verse 23). Thus they, like all the other forces, are the auxiliaries of Yahweh who wages this war and whose coming was extolled at the beginning of the song (verses 4 f.).

But was the battle by the waters of Megiddo also not an Israelite war? According to verse 13 it was "the people of Yahweh" [1] who "descended" to the battle; and that Israel

[1] Thus according to LXX[B], etc.; compare earlier verse 11.

13

is called the people of Yahweh is familiar from later passages of the Old Testament. That is generally assumed for our passage; indeed it has even been presumed that the word Israel was originally there.[2] But verse 13a also allows itself to be understood without so decisive a change, and thus it remains unlikely that the poet called the combatants Israel— however often the word Israel occurs elsewhere in the song. Also by no means did all the constituents of Israel participate in the battle. Ephraim, Benjamin, Machir, Zebulun, Issachar, and (textual emendation) Naphtali "descended."[3] The others did not come and thereby bear the critical derision of the poet: Reuben, Gilead, Dan, and Asher. Over against the Israel in action thus stands a potential Israel, and only the second of these in general bears the name Israel. One derives the second by adding the participants in the battle to the nonparticipants. This results in a total of ten names.

What is the importance of this sum? It is only certain that it included the constituents of Israel which, according to the opinion of the poet, might have come for the purpose of participating in the battle in question. A part of contemporary scholarship goes beyond this reliable statement. It retains the ten names for the names of the tribes which at that time had formed the amphictyony, the sacred confederation of the tribes of Israel. Thus the confederation at that

---

[2] In verse 13a parallel to the יהוה עם of the second half of the verse (see the previous footnote). Thus Moore at this passage and others.

[3] That all these tribes participated in the fight, and not only Zebulun and Naphtali as Judges 4:6, 10 states, seems to me historically the more likely. According to M. Noth, Judges 5 has conversely "expanded the circle of secondary parties concerned" (*The History of Israel*, p. 150, n. 3). However, Judges 5 is the older and also the more trustworthy source. That afterwards the circle of parties concerned was not expanded in the direction of a united Israel, as one can at first surmise according to many analogies, but on the contrary has been diminished (Judges 5:18 could have presented the pretext for the reduction down to Zebulun and Naphtali), conforms throughout to the doctrine of Yahweh war, which more likely demands a modest rather than a great military force on the part of Israel. Moreover, among the people in Judges 4, Jael has the principal role. For another solution, see A. Weiser, *ZAW*, 71 (1959), 84 ff.

time consisted not of twelve but of ten tribes.[4] The thesis is plausible because it is simple. However, it requires re-examination. At the same time we must keep in mind not only the number ten in its relation to the number twelve, but before all else the far more important general presupposition on which the thesis referred to is based, or which here intrudes upon it: namely that the war of Yahweh is an event of the amphictyony as such. According to G. v. Rad [5] "the emergence of the inclusive sacred alliance is the foremost characteristic of such a war," "these wars present themselves . . . in principle as a reaction of the amphictyony." If that is true, then we are able to view Israel between the taking of the land and the establishing of the state in existence and action, generally speaking, as a unity. Not that there had existed no tension between tribe and tribe, tribe and confederation. But the two great manifestations of national life, which go beyond the individual tribe and are collectively Israelite, or at least claim a collectively Israelite character, would to some extent be brought into congruity, even if not always in reality, at least in principle—and that would indeed be a great deal. The common denominator would be the cultic. For, according to almost universal agreement, the tribal confederation, which in this view had priority, was a cultic institution. Consequently, the Yahweh war should also be regarded "as an eminently cultic . . . undertaking." [6] One could not understand it "without knowing something of its cultic background." [7] Since the "cultic background," namely the amphictyony, is known to us, with it we would have in our hand the key to the understanding of the Yahweh war. Conversely, there would have been no possibility of this

---

[4] S. Mowinckel, *Von Ugarit nach Qumran* (*BZAW*, 77 [1958], 137); A. Weiser, *ZAW*, 71:87; against the fixed number of twelve. See also J. Hoftijzer, *Nederlands Theol. Tijdschr.*, 14 (1960), 255.

[5] *Der Heilige Krieg*, pp. 25-26. Similar remarks by other writers can be easily produced.

[6] v. Rad, *Der Heilige Krieg*, p. 14.

[7] *Ibid.*, p. 18.

understanding prior to the time of the amphictyony which is known to us; or there would be a possibility, but only if one had assumed an older cultic background of an amphictyonic kind.[8] With these propositions, whose consequences are greater than one might suppose upon first sight, the scope of our inquiry is set forth. Therefore the question is: Is it true that the Yahweh war is an event of the cultic tribal confederation?

First of all, there is the preliminary question concerning the names in the Song of Deborah. This causes some difficulty. The concept of an amphictyony is not firmly connected with ten tribes, apart from a few exceptions which can always be explained by peculiar circumstances, but with twelve tribes.[9] If one discards the number twelve, then the surest and most important *tertium comparationis* which we possess for the comparison between the Israelite tribal confederacy and the sacred confederations of ancient Greece is lost. Stated more plainly, this comparison then is senseless and inadmissible; it then is no longer permissible to describe Israel prior to the formation of the state with the concept of an amphictyony originally belonging to the Greek twelve-tribe (or six-tribe) confederation. Only the number twelve has made possible the comparison and permitted the inferences which can be drawn from it for Israel prior to the formation of the state. Consequently, anyone who considers the ten names which the Song of Deborah mentions as the entire list of a sacred tribal confederation may not appeal to Noth's book of 1930 to support this. He must attempt to construct such a confederation without the Greek analogy. It is very questionable whether that can be managed.

However, our question regarding the congruity of Yahweh war and tribal confederation has not been answered in the negative, not even for the battle of Deborah. It could indeed be that the ten names denoted, if not the entire tribal

---

[8] Compare *ibid.*, p. 17.
[9] Compare the evidence in the case of M. Noth, *System*, pp. 43 ff.

confederation, at least the portion of it capable of action. The Tribes of Judah and Simeon are missing. The adherents of the ten-tribe theory explain that these two tribes at that time did not belong to the tribal confederation, which later they unquestionably did. I assume here they were already members at that time.[10] That they do not appear in the song means with certainty that for participation in the battle they came so little into consideration that the poet did not consider it necessary to reprimand them for their absence. For that, a very plausible reason was cited long ago: the two tribes are isolated from the others by "the hostile belt of the south," [11] which the Canaanite city-states of Jerusalem, Gezer, Aijalon, and Shaalbim formed between the area of the Rachel tribes and that of Judah.[12] Naturally, one can say the poet, as he reprimanded Reuben, Gilead, Dan, and Asher for their absence, must also have explicitly deplored the absence of Judah and Simeon. However, this supposition is not convincing and for that reason is also not qualified to destroy the thesis of the amphictyonic character of the battle of Deborah. Since this is not done by the absence of the names of Judah and Simeon, neither is it convincingly done by the presence in the list of two names, Machir and Gilead, which in this form are not part of the lists familiar to us of the twelve tribes, respectively, the twelve sons of Jacob. They take the places which we find occupied in the familiar tribal lists by Manasseh and Gad. The correlation is at once clear; the difference need not disturb us in our context.[13] Thus among the names listed in the Song of Deborah, we have to deal with only a minor variant of those other lists. What is to be inferred now, with the above-mentioned restric-

[10] Compare R. Smend, *Gehörte Juda zum vorstaatlichen Israel?* (Proceedings of the Fourth World Congress of Jewish Studies, Jerusalem, 1965).

[11] K. Budde, *Das Buch der Richter (Kurzer Hand-Commentar zum Alten Testament,* VII [1897]), 40.

[12] Compare Judges 1:21, 29, 35 and in addition A. Alt, *Essays*, p. 166.

[13] On the complicated problem of the relationship between Gilead and Gad, compare most recently M. Noth *ZDPV*, 75 (1959), 14 ff.; J. Hoftijzer, *Nederlands Theol. Tijdschr.*, pp. 241 ff.

tions, from the coincidence of the circle of the Israelite amphictyonies and that of the potential participants in the battle
of Deborah? Surely, no coinciding between Yahweh war
and tribal confederation. This is proved by the inactive
standing apart of a considerable number of tribes and by the
fact that they were only rebuked with derision[14] and no
sanction was taken againt them.[15] The amphictyonic confederation as such is scarcely related to Yahweh war. If it had
been, then the refusal to participate would have been a breach
of the confederation and also would have been evaluated
differently in the song. However, with that the problem is not
solved. In the song something emerges which one can call
"amphictyonic will":[16] the will to refer the deed of the
smaller community to the large community to demonstrate
the Israel in action to the potential Israel, in order that
the potential Israel will one day become an Israel of action.
One cannot say for certain who the bearers of this amphictyonic will are. Perchance only the poet and the group to
which he belongs? Or one of the two parties involved—the
victor or the amphictyony: the victor in the battle missed
the cooperation of the others and included the complaint
about their lack of support on the roll of the members of
the amphictyony who were united through a common exer-
cise of the cult; or the amphictyony subsequently wished to
stamp the deed of the few as the deed of the entire confederation? [17] We do not know, because it cannot be determined
from the song. But this uncertainty is also among the reasons

[14] Weiser even supposed they were rather excused (*ZAW*, 71:88). On
volunteering, compare also H. J. Stoebe, *Festschrift F. Baumgärtel* (1959),
pp. 185-86.
[15] On the other hand, compare H. Bengtson, *Griechische Geschichte*
(*Handbuch der Altertumswissenschaft*, Vol. III, no. 4 [2nd ed., 1960]), p.
173, and the literature indicated therein.
[16] For the expression I am indebted to Professor Martin Buber in Jerusalem.
[17] This situation would be especially acknowledged if A. Weiser is correct
in saying that the Song of Deborah portrayed not the battle as such, but a
cultic dramatic presentation of it for a later solemn festival of the entire
tribal confederation (*ZAW*, 71:67 ff.) .

why one may not press the expression "amphictyonic will" in the sense that it is categorically a question of a tendency in direction toward the amphictyonic institution as it existed in former times. Categorically the will is collectively Israelite; it is amphictyonic inasmuch as it envisages the tribes which belong to the amphictyony (or those among them which are within reach).

The Song of Deborah is certainly the oldest source we possess for our inquiry, but by no means the only one. What we have, moreover, are, of course, later reflections in which the structure of what has taken place can be discerned with even less certainty than in the oldest source, which, as we saw, did not answer our questions quite so clearly as we would have wished. However, we possess nevertheless the criteria for evaluation, not only in the laws of historical probability, but also in the relation of the assertions of the later sources to the Song of Deborah. So there is still something which can be said.

It is beyond every doubt that, apart from the battle of Deborah, only single alliances participated in the Yahweh wars of the time of Judges, and not Israel as a whole.

Besides the people of Abiezer to whom he himself belonged, Gideon called upon all of Manasseh in addition to Asher, Zebulun, and Naphtali in the fight against the Midianites (Judges 6:34 f.). During the pursuit of the routed enemy, there occurred a new levy by which Naphtali, Asher, and all Manasseh were affected; there is nothing in the report concerning Zebulun (Judges 7:23). Ephraim was subsequently mentioned (verse 24). It is not quite clear how these assertions relate to each other and to the entire account. Possibly 6:35 is an addition;[18] perhaps also 7:23.[19] Then at first, not several tribes but only the people of Abiezer were

[18] According to v. Rad, *Der Heilige Krieg*, p. 22, it is a question of an exaggerating addition.

[19] The tribes do nothing in verses 24 f. according to Budde, *Das Buch der Richter*, p. 62. Verse 24 with regard to 8:1-3 is indispensable.

summoned,[20] and by the end Ephraim as well was participating (or, with the retention of 7:23, also Naphtali, Asher,
and all of Manasseh).

The army at whose head Jephthah fought against the
Ammonites is purely Gileadite (Judges 11). A coalition with
Judah, Benjamin, and Ephraim is not very likely in view of
the complete silence concerning these tribes in the report
about the battle and its preparations and can hardly be inferred [21] "from Judges 10:9 in connection with 12:1." [22]

One may also place the Benjaminite Ehud on the side of
Barak, Gideon, and Jephthah. Even if in his story "the Israelites" are mentioned (Judges 3:15, 27), the context at least
is obvious, so that one has only to reckon in the first phase
(verse 15) with Benjaminites, in the second (verse 27) moreover with the Ephraimites.

The above instances concur in that the designation of the
participating tribes has not succeeded in being exact, but
even so, in any case, it is fundamentally correct. The Deuteronomic framework, with its expansion to Israel as a whole,
is nowhere able to conceal it completely. The insight into its
secondary character may, on the other hand, lead us to attach
little value beyond the individual tribe to the feature which
is already discernible here everywhere in the old accounts
and which conforms throughout on a smaller scale with what
the Song of Deborah asserts in this respect. Its elementary
form is the call for help, by which the group that at any given
time was threatened sounded a summons to arms among one
or the other or even several neighbors in addition to its own
people; this is denoted by the Hebrew through the verb
זעק/צעק (qal and hiphil; passive niphal). It occurs before the
beginning of the battle (Judges 4:10; 6:35; 12:2; compare

---

[20] Supporting this is 8:2b.

[21] 10:9 is Deuteronomic (compare Noth, *Überlieferungsgeschichtliche
Studien,* p. 53); and the mention of a fruitless conscription of Ephraim
by Jephthah in 12:2 "is not altogether convincing" (v. Rad, *Der Heilige
Krieg,* p. 23, n. 34).

[22] Buber, *Königtum,* p. 127, n. 43.

8:1) or before its final event (7:23 f.; compare 3:27). At the same time no distinction existed in the expression between the levy of one's own group and that of the others (compare 6:34 with 35). A tribe could also be offended at times if it were not immediately called upon for help; so Ephraim (Judges 8:1-3; 12:1-6 [23]). This cry for help to the neighbor—which in the present text is drowned out by the cry which, according to the Deuteronomist's account, the Israelites were always raising to Yahweh (Judges 3:15 etc.) — and the results achieved by it are the most unquestionable, the most essential, and the most vital manifestation of Israelite unity which is known to us from that time. Therein an "amphictyonic sense of solidarity" [24] might be involved; the proceedings, however, give no occasion for speaking of a "general amphictyonic interest" [25] or even an "amphictyonic concern." [26] The levy is determined by the actual military requirement; that it affects the groups that also worship the god Yahweh, and thus as they cried for help belonged to the amphictyony, is self-evident by the character of this war. Israel as a whole, however, not to mention the amphictyonic institution, does not appear. It is certainly not different from the Song of Deborah, but rather even clearer than in the Song of Deborah.[27]

[23] As for the relation of the two passages, compare E. Täubler, *Biblische Studien* (1958), p. 293 and the literature indicated there; more recently M. Noth, *ZDPV*, 75 (1959), 61, n. 113.

[24] v. Rad, *Der Heilige Krieg*, p. 22 (concerning Ehud).

[25] *Ibid.*, p. 23 (concerning Gideon).

[26] *Ibid.*, p. 24 (concerning Jephthah).

[27] By comparison the question intrudes itself: To which tribes might the levy have been issued before the battle of Deborah? It scarcely allows an answer. After the relative clemency which the song exercises in relation to four nonparticipating units, one could be inclined to assume that only the six tribes were called upon which had then in fact participated and that the view toward the four others was a more or less theoretical reflection following the deed from an almost collective Israelite point of view. For a more positive judgment, we lack the criteria. Meroz appears to have felt the duty to help; was it perchance summoned in the final phase of the battle (for which we had an example above) for the pursuit of the defeated enemy?

Unfortunately we cannot date the battle by the waters of Megiddo. The comparison with the presupposed situations [28] in the other accounts of Judges yields little, and the excavation of Megiddo nothing at all since the city was not affected by the battle.[29] Nevertheless, this much is certain: that the taking of the land in all its stages was concluded.[30] Thus we may think of a time which lies not too long before the establishing of the state and in any case is nearer to this than to the formation of the tribal alliances. The question in our context is not entirely an idle one, and for that reason it is doubly unfortunate that we cannot answer it more precisely. The Song of Deborah indeed towers above the old accounts of the book of Judges referred to in that it treats of greater dimensions and thinks in them: more Israelite tribes took part in the battle than anywhere else in the book, and then it is even deplored that these are not enough. Certainly there is a militarily strategic basis for that: the Canaanite war-chariot might in the plain requires a larger body of men than the nomads who attacked from the east. Perhaps this reason clears up everything so far. Apart from reasons that are purely pragmatic and related to the situation, it is natural to understand the view of the Song of Deborah toward the whole of Israel in terms of relations which go beyond the particularity of the battles of the Judges which until now we have considered exclusively. The question then reads: In the Song of Deborah have we to do with a remnant of an original all-Israelite amphictyonic combat association, or instead with the germ cell—no, more: an already advanced stage of the political development of all Israel? Does the view extend backward or forward?

When not read very critically, the Old Testament is not acquainted with this alternative. Under Moses and Joshua Israel traveled and fought in the totality of its twelve tribes.

---

[28] Most recently, Täubler, *Biblische Studien*, p. 164.

[29] A. Alt, *Kleine Schriften*, I, 266, n. 2; Noth, *History*, p. 151, n. 1.

[30] Dan already seems to be in the north; compare Alt, *Kleine Schriften*, I, 160 and n. 5. On the other hand, Machir still stands in the place of Manasseh.

Then comes the time in which the war reveals itself to the discerning reader to be sectional and to which belongs the Song of Deborah, which—even though impotently—aims at the whole of Israel. Finally, Israel again stands under Saul as such. The sequence is like a broad river which suddenly divides itself into twelve streams which flow along a lengthy distance separated from each other, only later to rejoin the old river. The comparison does not hold in every respect, but perhaps the impossibility of the picture already projects a light upon the comparable matter.

As is well known, the political-military unity of Israel before and during the taking of the land does not withstand criticism. It did not exist; the proof of this fact need no longer be cited.[31] A united Israel was not yet involved in the events in the desert upon the departure from Egypt; and Palestine was not conquered as the book of Joshua describes it, in one expedition of military power under the command of Joshua, but on the contrary, successively by isolated groups and tribes and without having regularly employed military power to any great extent at the beginning. It is highly probable that Israel established itself as such, in the form familiar to us, for the first time on the soil of arable land. That no consolidation thereupon ensued for combined military action is no surprise, considering the geographical location; the plain and certain groups of cities remained mostly in the possession of the previous inhabitants and therewith divided the tribes into several groups, between which military communication must have been difficult. Though the military particularism of the time of Judges was required by the circumstances, it appears on the other hand to have been sufficient to meet the military problem: ability and enthusiasm of a tribe or small tribal groups were mostly sufficient to deal with the eastern neighbors. Of course, where it involved

---

[31] Compare Alt, *Kleine Schriften*, I, 126 ff.; *Essays*, pp. 133 ff.; Noth, *History*, pp. 69 ff.; v. Rad, *Der Heilige Krieg*, pp. 15 ff.

a coalition of "the kings of Canaan," there it required greater forces than usual. They were summoned and obtained. The event had to influence deeply the collective Israelite consciousness. There are "massacres just like that extolled in the Song of Deborah which denote the intrinsic development of the national idea." [32] From there it is not far to the Philistine menace which produced the joint summons to arms of all tribes and the state of Israel.

We cannot fix this last point in time in the Old Testament tradition with complete exactness. Was the whole of Israel already involved in the Philistine battles which stand behind the story of the Ark in I Samuel 4–6? [33] Probably the first convocation of Israelite levies is described in I Samuel 11, where, strange to say, the opponents were not the Philistines but the Ammonites. Was Saul, first of all, testing the troops of the levies on the smaller opponent? Or did the Philistine war, in which only Benjamin and then Ephraim (compare 14:23 LXX) seem to participate, belong chronologically prior to the Ammonite campaign? [34] Also, the saga of I Samuel 11 is in itself difficult for the historian to utilize. Its logic requires that the future king send his messenger בכל־גבול ישראל and that the people then come out "as one man" (verse 7). "This event cannot have occurred so entirely poetically in reality, but the story bears no pragmatizing and must be left as it is." [35] We have supposed that Saul at that time was backed by less than Deborah and Barak, perhaps as much as Gideon and Jephthah, hence his own tribe and perhaps the nearest neighbors.[36] But it does not exclude the previous summons to all tribes. Nevertheless, through

[32] A. Bertholet, *Kulturgeschichte Israels* (1919), p. 104.

[33] So Noth, *History*, p. 165, with a reference to the participation of the Ark which in my opinion is not unconditionally valid (see Chap. IV below).

[34] So Ed. Meyer, *Geschichte des Altertums*, Vol. II, no. 2 (3rd ed., 1953), p. 245; compare also Alt, *Essays*, p. 191, n. 46.

[35] Wellhausen, *Geschichte*, p. 52, n. 1.

[36] J. Pedersen, *Israel*, III/IV (1940), 43. Compare besides, v. Rad, *Der Heilige Krieg*, p. 20 and n. 27; Noth, *History*, p. 168.

Saul's kingdom and that which it brought with it, the sectionalism was broken, and the all-Israelite levy, if not already immediately a reality, was then indeed only a question of time.

In the foregoing, though so to speak only statistically, we have prepared the answer to the question regarding the relation between Yahweh war and tribal confederation, as it was revealed to us in the Song of Deborah and there could only be provisionally answered. It concerned itself with the outer, not inner side; with the number, not the substance. But now it is no ordinary war with which we are concerned but the war of Yahweh, and no ordinary alliance of tribe to a nation but a sacred confederation. It is clear that only the comparison of the natures of the two phenomena can supply the answer to our question. But a certain preliminary judgment has no doubt already revealed itself: the two entities do not actually agree statistically. One can trace this back carefully to the weight of outside circumstances which would have destroyed an originally intended and essential unity or no doubt impeded its initial development. But this would only be the admission that it had been from the outset a question of a hardly viable, indeed strictly speaking, an unhistorical structure.[37] We must conclude, however, from the facts that strong arguments are needed in order to counterbalance at least the prevailing circumstantial evidence and thus to prove the Yahweh war to be an undertaking of the tribal confederation.

[37] Compare on this point v. Rad, *Der Heilige Krieg*, p. 28.

2

Military Event and Cultic Institution

Perhaps nothing throws so bright a light upon the diverse character of Yahweh war and tribal confederation as the fact that the Old Testament knows of one, speaks of it and describes it, but to all intents and purposes, not the other. The expression "war of Yahweh" was itself produced above entirely from the content of the Song of Deborah, and just as naturally it is suggested by the descriptions of warlike events of a similar nature. As for the wording, it can also appeal to the Old Testament which knows the apparently firmly fixed formula of the מלחמות יהוה (I Samuel 18:17; 25: 28; compare 17:47) and even quotes from a ספר מלחמות יהוה (Numbers 21:14). Whether the designation is now especially used or not, the Israelites who speak to us in the Old Testament have, at all stages and of their history, an extremely active conception of war and the wars of Yahweh. Its occurrence stamped itself upon them in a drastic fashion; the memory was not lost. It was often affirmed and could also illustrate the hope of the future (Isaiah 9:3). The dynamic force of the conception also shows itself in that it could transform the old traditions of the taking of the land in Palestine by the Israelites, or even form them altogether anew. The latter is also true of the confederation of the tribes, but in a quite different sense. While the phenomenon of the war of Yahweh was an actively preserved conception, only the substratum of a common unity of the twelve tribes under the name Israel remained of the confederation of tribes. Afterwards, it penetrated everywhere and saturated and superim-

26

posed the old traditions to such an extent that they can only seldom be separated from it without harm. As certain as the necessity of this solution is to the historian, it seems scarcely possible to the historian of tradition, since the unity of Israel is almost without exception a presupposition of the formation of tradition as far as it can still be traced. To see the reality behind the substratum of tribal unity here is very difficult, because it is, unlike the war of Yahweh, obviously no longer known[1] to the writers of the Old Testament and was only again discovered by modern scholarship by means of inference and analogy. The names which were given to it—confederation,[2] league, amphictyony—are unknown to the Old Testament and belong originally to the analogous phenomena of other nations where we find the reality, and not merely a meager substratum, still in the sources. Thus, the tribal confederation is nothing more than a hypothesis, even if a probable one. It has a good basis.

"It was . . . above all the necessity of history in which Israel became conscious of itself and Yahweh. The climax of history in those days and for centuries to come was the war. Israel means *El fights,* and Yahweh was the fighting El after whom the people named itself. The war camp was the cradle of the nation, it was also the oldest sanctuary. Israel was there and Yahweh was there. Whereas in times of rest both fell asleep together, so they were again disturbed through the danger of an enemy; the awakening of Israel always began then with that of Yahweh. Yahweh aroused the men who, driven by the spirit, put themselves at the head of the people; his own leadership was personified in them. Yahweh moved out among the warriors of the levy; in their enthusiasm his presence could be felt. Finally Yahweh decided from the heavens the fight which was conducted on earth. He always stood on the side of Israel; his interest was confined to

[1] Compare Noth, *Überlieferungsgeschichtliche Studien,* p. 95, n. 1.
[2] The word ברית is not used in this sense, to say nothing of the special case intended here.

Israel, even if his power—to that end he was God—extended far beyond the borders of the nation. Thus Yahweh in reality was a *living* God, but manifestations of his activity in the great crises of history were interrupted by long pauses. There was something tempestuous about his effectiveness; it was better suited for extraordinary situations than for everyday use." [3]

Therewith the war of Yahweh is described as what one could term the dynamic principle of the earliest history and history of the religion of Israel. In an extraordinary manner, it is event, action and deed. Hence the impression which overshadows everything else and the enduring memory; hence the powerful effect; hence, also, a necessary one-sidedness. There is no existence, neither religious nor national, which only subsists in climaxes, especially when these climaxes lie far apart. Therefore, the old accounts of the war, when they are taken out of context and reassembled, produce no total picture of Israel of the time which they portray. They do not tell what happened between the wars in the years, the number of which the Deuteronomist indicates as forty, but during which he can only report that Israel had peace with its enemies (Judges 3:11, etc.). What we hear nothing of is the static alongside the dynamic, the continuing alongside the unique; more precisely put, the institutional. That nothing can be read *expressis verbis* respecting it in the Old Testament does not prove it did not exist. For that, we rightly tend to cite the reason that the constant or the ordinary, because it is obvious and generally well known, need not be described. It is more important that the understanding and presentation of what was static as static runs counter to the laws of the earlier writing of history in the Old Testament. Situations and relations are regularly re-thought into events and are described by the telling of these events, in which telling we can distinguish a paradigmatic and an etiological style. In case of changes in the situations and relationships,

---

[3] J. Wellhausen, *Skizzen und Vorarbeiten,* I (1884), 10-11.

the narratives which refer to them need not fall into disuse.
They can be placed before a new background within which
their sense is shifted accordingly. After what has been said,
the silence of the Old Testament concerning the institutional counterpart to the war of Yahweh by no means refutes its
existence,[4] but no doubt it is an eloquent testimony for the
structural difference of the two entities.

Old Testament scholarship, the more strongly it was influenced by inquiries oriented to the "static" aspect—thus
by sociological inquiries—has increasingly devoted its attention to the institution in question. Today only outsiders
neglect it.[5] Even for Wellhausen there was no pressing problem here. He brought the Israel which came into action at the
climactic points of history into the sociological category of a
"warlike league," [6] but waived an analogous designation for
the Israel of the peaceful intervening times. It would likely
have seemed absurd to him. For "Israel is no ordinary organ-
ism to whose regular functions belonged the conducting of
war; Israel is only an idea," an idea, to be sure, which in the
war of Yahweh—and Yahweh is more than just an idea!—
takes on a highly realistic form.[7] Max Weber took over the
expression, "league," and applied it also to that from which
Wellhausen had withheld it: to the Israel between the wars.[8]
He spoke of a "confederation of war under and with Yahweh
as the war god of the confederacy, guarantor of its social
orders and creator of the material well-being of the league." [9]
The advance beyond Wellhausen in this respect is certainly
less in today's view than one might at first suppose. Weber

[4] Compare on this point, Noth, *System*, pp. 64-65.

[5] Thus for Täubler, *Biblische Studien*, p. 1, the time of the Judges is
simply "the epoch of the independent tribes"; the "real or unreal genealogical
bond of the tribes" cited by him later on turns out to have no institutional
significance for him.

[6] *Geschichte*, p. 23.

[7] *Ibid.*, p. 37.

[8] *Gesammelte Aufsätze zur Religionssoziologie*, III (1921), 90 ff.

[9] *Ibid.*, p. 90.

concludes from the absence of permanent political organs, common jurisdiction, unified administration, and a priesthood of the confederation, that the unity of the confederation was existent only in the war [10] and was expressed in "that a war hero or war prophet accredited by Yahweh also regularly claimed authority beyond the borders of his tribe." [11] Therewith an explanation of the unity of Israel in the time prior to the state is fundamentally relinquished; indeed, this unity itself is abandoned. For, as we have seen above, the unity of Israel in the time prior to the state did not appear *per se* in the war. Certainly, common war experience may have strengthened the coherence of the tribes actually participating—but there were never many; also, the human leader in the war may have still retained authority over this group afterwards—but that did not last long. Weber's conception, therefore, breaks down at a very important point. The reason lies in the fact that Weber, just as Wellhausen before him, reckoned with, as defective as it may be, a total Israel which was already acting unitedly in political and military matters under Moses in the desert, as the continuation or echo of which one could understand the military association of single tribes in the fertile land. [12] The question poses itself differently, since that is no longer possible, and therewith the problem of the relationship between Yahweh war and tribal confederation has also been shifted and intensified—indeed, rather, is actually posed for the first time.

One does not have to go so far as to say the Yahweh war did not mean anything for Israel's consciousness of unity. Politically Israel became a unity through the Philistine war (or already in the Ammonite war), and the older wars have

[10] *Ibid.*, pp. 92, 146, 173.

[11] *Ibid.*, p. 92.

[12] An important source of error is also that Weber did not distinguish the execution of the confederation in Judges 19-20 (which will be dealt with later on) from the Yahweh war and for that reason sees Yahweh war partly in the light of the confederation; compare *ibid.*, pp. 52, 98.

afforded the people the most essential components of what one could call its national myth; and with that myth, as with the experience mediated through it of joint action of single tribal groups, of which we have already spoken, the older wars certainly exerted an integrating influence which one may not treat lightly. The application to Israel [13] of the principal of the war which creates the nations is scarcely assailable, not even with the thesis that "the originality of the warlike tendency of the religion of Yahweh does not withstand a closer examination"; [14] on the contrary, this thesis in its generalization scarcely proves correct.[15] Also against the previously quoted proposition of Bertholet concerning the wars of Yahweh as the "true progress of a national idea" [16] nothing can be said; it remains correct. But such accuracies easily conceal the problem which lies in the fact that we cannot explain the unity of all Israel, as it is shown to us (it matters little about the exact limits) in the Song of Deborah in the potential and with Saul in action, from the necessities and experiences of the war of Yahweh prior to the creation of the state. It is quite obvious that such an explanation is urgently desirable and would be the most important service that could have been rendered by the hypothesis of the "warlike league" or the "confederation of men" which had the conducting of wars as its main task.[17] It does not render it. One may therefore speak of leagues or confederations of men which are created *ad hoc* out of this or that tribe, perhaps also of earlier alliances of that kind as a model, or subsequent alliance as a result—we do not know anything about that—but the notion that prior to the formation of the state an Israel in its totality and continuity

[13] Wellhausen, *Geschichte*, p. 23.

[14] W. Caspari, *Die Gottesgemeinde vom Sinaj und das nachmalige Volk Israel*. Discussions with Max Weber (*Beiträge zur Förderung christlicher Theologie*, Vol. 72, no. 1 [1922]) , p .15.

[15] Compare H. Fredriksson, *Jahwe als Krieger* (1945) , and pp. 41-42 below.

[16] *Kulturgeschichte Israels*, p. 104.

[17] For that, see Caspari, *Die Gottesgemende vom Sinaj*, pp. 14 ff.

is to be comprehended under such categories should be discarded.[18]

Thus with the rejection of the leagues formed *ad hoc,* of an enduring joint political-military institution, and of a unity of all Israel prior to the taking of the land as explanatory grounds for the phenomena referred to of uniform challenge and action, there remains only a collective institution[19] of a character decidedly different from a political-military one, indeed one without important functions of that kind.[20] This is precisely the tribal confederation which Noth postulated in 1930. Its existence, as was already pointed out, is not provable. Arguing for it, however, is not only the above mentioned conclusion,[21] but also the fact that from this perspective the element of Old Testament tradition concerning the twelve tribes of Israel—and that is without any doubt

---

[18] For that, compare *ibid.,* p. 82: "It can still be maintained that the collective nationality, which had to produce the state, became conscious of itself through the wars and in that way became crystallized. But therewith one deprives himself of the claim to the further contention that the wars were already conducted for the sake of this nationality. Subsequently indeed they were; however, we are not concerned here with these but with the wars of the Yahweh believers prior to the formation of the state. The armies in these wars were occasional followers. They were not yet a nation in arms. One would move in a circle if one were to look upon the people as the source of the summons to arms and then upon the national consciousness as the consequence of the campaign.

[19] To think of non-institutional data (the "Yahwism," the "common religious possession," etc.) as some liked to do in earlier times and still do, is prohibited, because in doing so, it essentially has always been based upon the institutional unity of all Israel, even prior to the taking of the land, as an initial presupposition. Compare further what has been said in principle against such non-institutional general conceptions by Noth, *System,* pp. 62-63.

[20] An impossible structure has been presupposed by J. Hempel, *Gott und Mensch im Alten Testament* (2nd ed., 1936), p. 37, where it is said: "The confederation cultus serves the goal of guaranteeing the military aid of the god for the 'league' through magic decree and saving action." Could the confederation cultus be constantly attuned to a military situation—which on the whole was a rarity? Or was it not present in times of peace? But how could one again revive it in time in case of war when one must act with the greatest speed? Moreover, M. Weber's league, on the other hand, also does not become any more intelligible by virtue of the fact that he designates it here and there as a cultic confederation (*Gesammelte Aufsätze zur Religionssoziologie,* pp. 90, 98).

[21] Noth, *System,* pp. 62 ff.

thought of as totally Israelite—can be satisfactorily understood; [22] the tradition for its part furnishes the extremely important analogy in connection with other nations and also
the possibility of compensating for the missing Old Testament accounts concerning the Israelite confederation of
tribes, with due reservation and in accordance with what the
Old Testament in other respects reports on the time prior
to the state.[23]

What provides the analogy for our inquiry? The Greek
amphictyonies about which we are best informed were, according to common opinion, cultic-sacral alliances. They
could also achieve political effect, but that was not the rule
and came, if at all, later and secondarily.[24] Extraordinary
circumstances were required in order to allow the political
elements to outweigh the sacred.[25] That is precisely the case
with the confederation of the twelve Etruscan cities.[26]

Now to be sure, once in awhile the war also had its place
in the life of the Greek amphictyony. The "holy wars," of
which the pylaic-delphic amphictyony conducted several,
absolutely cannot be compared with the war of Yahweh.[27]
They are rather the most extreme form of criminal procedure
against violators of the amphictyonic law. They were preceded by proper processes in which the facts were ascertained and the execution agreed upon. Not only were the

[22] *Ibid.*, pp. 3 ff.

[23] *Ibid.*, pp. 42 ff.

[24] Unfortunately, a more recent monograph about the Greek amphictyonies
is missing. Compare in place of that, in addition to *ibid.*, p. 55 and the
bibliography given there on p. 47, n. 5, H. E. Stier, *Grundlagen und Sinn der
griechischen Geschichte* (1945), pp. 123-24, and the bibliography provided
there; Ed. Meyer, *Geschichte des Altertums*, III (3rd ed., 1954) 327; H. Berve,
Griechische Frühzeit (1959), pp. 105-6; H. Bengtson, *Griechische Geschichte*
(*Handbuch der Altertumswissenschaft*, Vol. III, no. 4 [2nd ed., 1960]) pp.
84-85.

[25] That was the case with the Ionic city states. That this however was
plainly a political establishment (so Wilamowitz) has been contested. Compare L. Ziehen, *RE*, Vol. 36, no. 2 (1949) column 602.

[26] O. W. v. Vacano, *Die Etrusker* (1955), pp. 63 ff.; *Die Etrusker in der
Welt der Antike* (1957), pp. 42 ff., 50 ff.

[27] Rather comparable, perhaps, with A. Moser, *ThZ*, 16 (1960), 133-34.

member states affected, but also individual persons. The motives were not only, strictly speaking, of a sacred nature—that
is, violations of holy areas, etc.—but also transgressions of
international scope which were perpetrated against another
member of the amphictyony and therewith violated the oath
which the members had to swear and the fulfillment of which
the amphictyonic alliance had to control.[28] It is quite obvious
and has long been noted [29] that the Old Testament parallel
to this is to be found in what is said in Judges 19-20—that
is, in the joint warlike action of the tribes of Israel against
Benjamin which had sinned against a law that was valid in
all Israel. The dissimilarity to the Yahweh wars is great and
not to be smoothed over. Whereas there "everywhere appear
only the individual families and tribes or changing alliances
of the same, Israel here is completely centralized, a unified
machine. As one man they become angry, gather, deliberate
and resolve, weep and moan. . . . The unity of Israel is a
churchly one, the acting subject is the assembly of the people
of God (20:2) or, as the common expression goes, the congregation; . . . for עדה in the technical sense is no political
but a sacred congregation." [30] Wellhausen concludes from
this that the narrative is completely unhistorical: "as if the
twelve-division had ever had practical meaning and actual
existence," and "as if at that time thousands of sacred alliances did not exist, but only a single one"—thus Israel acts
here. The presuppositions of the narrative are therewith in
fact precisely described. Only we today consider them to be
historically given,[31] which Wellhausen was a long way from
doing. With that it is not said that the action against Benjamin must have been historical. Without any doubt there
is at least quite a bit in it which is legendary, and one has

---

[28] Compare esp. Cauer, *RE*, Vol. I, no. 2 (1894), columns 1917 ff., 1935;
also G. Busolt-H. Swoboda, *Griechische Staatskunde* (*Handbuch der Altertumswissenschaft*, Vol. IV, no. 1 [1st ed., 1926]), pp. 1293-94.

[29] Noth, *System*, pp. 101 ff.

[30] J. Wellhausen, *Composition*, p. 229.

[31] Naturally, the second cannot be circumscribed quite as exactly.

to abandon in any case some particulars and also some of the color of the whole,[32] if one[33] wishes to retain an essential historical point. But this is not crucial for our inquiry. It is enough that we see how a "holy war in the amphictyonic sense," [34] a "confederation war" [35] had to appear.

Yet one other cultic military venture of which the Old Testament reports can be contrasted with the old Yahweh wars: the wonderful victory of King Jehoshaphat over Moab and Ammon according to II Chronicles 20. Here again the main point is not the possible historical background,[36] but instead what v. Rad[37] calls "spiritual sublimation." More explicitly than is elsewhere common, it is emphasized that it is Yahweh who fights the war (verses 15, 17, 29), and thus one could think here Yahweh war of the old style had once more arisen. But the great cultic apparatus which the narrator proclaims on earth forms the singular and bizarre elaboration. Where once upon a time someone appointed by Yahweh rose up and drew the warriors with him, at this point the king now organizes a fasting and a great gathering of the community in the outer court of the temple with prayer and a detailed, propitious oracle. On the next day after the martial sermon of the king, the Levites who go before the warriors in holy adornment need only to sing for an instant "Yahweh be thanked, for his mercy endures forever," and already the entire battle is fought without the striking of one Judaic blow, and the plundering lasting three days can begin. The fourth day is the time for the thanksgiving service, and finally the venture finds its conclusion in the Jerusalem Temple. The old motifs are pres-

---

[32] Compare the critique of Wellhausen, *Composition,* pp. 229 ff.
[33] With Noth, *System,* p. 170.
[34] Buber, *Königtum,* p. 127, n. 42.
[35] Noth, *History,* p. 105.
[36] Compare in addition M. Noth, *ZDPV,* 67 (1944/45) , 45 ff.; W. Rudolph in the same place.
[37] *Der Heilige Krieg,* p. 80.

ent,[38] but are extremely coarsened and distorted. The war of
Yahweh has become a great cultic venture operated according
to strict regulations; "the old original war cry (תרועה) has
been converted into a hymn of praise of an official group of
the cultic personnel." [39]

It is not that the cultic element in general had been missing from the war of Yahweh in ancient time. From the
outset that is not to be anticipated, because indeed it is
already by name a question of a religious event and, as such,
cultic forms in one way or another are almost always involved. In our case it is primarily a question of the consecration prior to and the ban after the battle, secondarily of
obtaining the oracle before the battle, in the presence of
which, however, the cultic character is quite often faded.[40]
At the same time, one may reflect upon occasional sacrificing,
blessing, and curse, or perhaps upon the fact that Barak,
according to Judges 4:6, 12, with the tribes of Naphtali and
Zebulun, moved to Mt. Tabor where there seems to have
been a not unimportant sanctuary at which some cultic preparations for the battle were made.[41] In this and similar lines
one can presume still more without attaining certainty. Over
against this is the fact that, even with the inclusion of the
undoubtedly present and important cultic elements, the war
of Yahweh as such and as a whole can hardly be subsumed
under the category of the cultic. It is not just that the whole
cultic community of Israel does not appear (and cannot appear) and that the amphictyonic institution is not participating (which is yet to be examined below); but moreover the
priests are not essentially prominent, and what there is of
cultic usage is the preparation which occurs in consecration

[38] Compare also G. Wilda, *Das Königsbild des chronistischen Geschichts-
werkes* (Dissertation, Evangelical Theological Faculty, Bonn, 1959), p. 74
and n. 16.

[39] v. Rad, *Der Heilige Krieg*, p. 81.

[40] The proof by v. Rad, pp. 7-8, 13.

[41] Perhaps the above mentioned consecration of the warriors. The oracle
was indeed already given through Deborah.

for a completely uncultic historical action of unique and incomparable force; and then there is the ban, the last discharge of this action, the non-military aspect of the human share in the action of Yahweh which is accompanying music and by no means the chief item.[42] But even the accompanying music has much improvisation; the wild, charismatic character of Yahweh war cannot attain to the orderly regularity which is otherwise the distinguishing mark of the cultus. Certainly a "theory of the holy war" [43] develops in the midst of and following the event. But in so doing there is much schematization and stiffness of form; and if one assumes this position, one has to state that the event "in its essential and intended form has historically never fully appeared." [44] It can be asked, therefore, if one can call the war of Yahweh a "sacred institution in the full sense of the word" or an "eminently cultic celebration, viz. conventionalized by fixed, traditional, sacred rites and performances." [45] Naturally one must, if one ascribes to the cultus also the "jurisdiction of the historical rule of Yahweh." [46] But not everything which concerns not the individual but the community is cultus,[47] and so one, to be sure, should not associate the war of Yahweh in its essence with the cultus—it may also be purely out of the compulsion of man to participate in the event and to master it intellectually and to revive this participation and accomplishment again in a later situation that a variety of cultic forms have crystallized about it and thus "the war camp" may have been "the oldest sanctuary." [48] In the words of the Song of Miriam in Exodus 15:21b, which

[42] The dominant feature here is the "freedom and incalculability of Yahweh" (v. Rad, Der Heilige Krieg, p. 31) .

[43] Ibid., pp. 6 ff.

[44] Ibid., p. 29, also p. 14.

[45] Ibid., pp. 6, 14.

[46] Ibid., p. 31.

[47] Contrary to ibid.

[48] One may under no circumstances conclude from this comment of Wellhausen (Geschichte, p. 24) that he understood the war of Yahweh in its entirety as a cultic celebration.

speaks solely of the power and action of Yahweh, the main point of the war of Yahweh is plainly stated—we are dealing here with a complete hymn; the declaration of the hymn is naturally capable of amplification, but clearly from the outset not necessarily in need of it—and where it occurs, just as in the Song of the Sea, here the main theme is only further pursued and executed, but nothing is said of the accompanying cultic phenomena. The event is chiefly and primarily "the war of Yahweh," only secondarily "holy war." [49] Its second aspect became prominent and developed primarily later when the event no longer occurred and the theory enjoyed a free hand. We have the end product before us in II Chronicles 20 where the cultic officials so behave "that the divine help is linked together precisely with the beginning of their cultic activity." [50] Here, despite the intense climax of what borders upon the miraculous, "the deity divested of mystery," [51] the origin is farthest removed.

Where the two most important forms of expression of the relationship between God and people confront each other— as institution and event, rest and awakening, normal cultic mediacy and non-cultic unfathomable immediacy, potential and action, continuous co-existence of the multitudes, brief association of the few—there, as much as all such contrasting pairs are to be taken *cum grano salis,* one may speak of a dualism, be it then again *cum grano salis.* Opposition both to an overly rigid use of this category, and also to the more enticing temptation to proceed further from here with Hegel, is provided by historical reality insofar as we can still recog-

---

[49] I utilize, therefore, in the text under discussion, the first expression (supported by Dr. S. Talmon in Jerusalem). The second has certainly prevailed, esp. through the books of Schwally and v. Rad, to such an extent that it will generally remain with us. It had its place originally in Greece (therefore, it could be applied to Judges 19-20) and then in Islam. Compare in addition also W. Caspari, *ZWTh,* 54 (1912), 148; W. Richter, *Traditionsgeschichtliche Untersuchungen zum Richterbuch (BBB,* 18 [1963]), p. 186; Th. C. Vriezen, *De godsdienst van Israël* (1963), pp. 134-35.

[50] v. Rad, *Der Heilige Krieg,* p. 81.

[51] Wellhausen, *Prolegomena,* p. 242.

nize it.[52] The fact that this dualism is not absolute it shares with all related structures of history, and just so, that in it dwells a special depth of history, that in its sphere of interest "the exciting" has to occur. "The crisis of the time of the Judges contained" the "paradox of the inner antithesis that an anarchical spiritual foundation has to support the structure of the absolute theocracy," says Buber;[53] by the "anarchical spiritual foundation" he means the "as it were, institutional interregna," the amphictyonic time which used to be politically a time of confusion, and by the "absolute theocracy" he means the Israel which appeared in the war of Yahweh.

To the presuppositions of the "crisis" belongs in addition to the antithesis also the mutuality. The old sources are certainly not completely in the wrong when they no longer know and report anything of the dualism, when in them on the one hand united Israel pushes the sectionalism so far into the background, and on the other hand the Yahweh war does the same with the sacred tribal confederation that we have trouble in pulling the two threads apart. In principle, if as a rule only there, the participants were indeed the same. Yahweh is the god of Yahweh war and of the amphictyony. Indeed, in the Song of Deborah he is being praised with the name יהוה אלהי ישראל (Judges 5:3, 5), which is in a special way connected with Shechem, the principal site of the amphictyony.[54] Certainly he does not come in his role as the god of the amphictyony; he comes not from Shechem but from Sinai (verse 5). But because Yahweh is there, in some sense Israel is also there. The צעקה of the threatened tribe is relevant for the neighboring tribe which also worships the god Yahweh and therefore also belongs to the amphictyony. Thereby the first takes precedence unconditionally over the

[52] Compare the corresponding endeavor with regard to the New Testament by J.-L. Leuba, *L'institution et l'événement* (1950) and in addition E. Käsemann's critique, *Verkündigung und Forschung 1956/57* (1957/59), pp. 163 ff.

[53] *Königtum*, p. 148.

[54] Compare C. Steuernagel, *BZAW*, 27 (1914), 329 ff.

second, for it is indeed the war of Yahweh and not the war
of the amphictyony. But because Yahweh is "no tribal god,
but the god of 'Israel,' " [55] his war is surely in principle
also a war of Israel—and such a principle was capable of
being more and producing more than one can realize from
the external circumstances and also more than one can quite
know. The war of Yahweh "was by its very nature the common war and the war of the commonwealth. . . . Of course
there are in the book of Judges only ventures of short-lived
or continuing alliances of a few tribes which are so reported;
but for the narrator—not just for the redactor—at any given
time Israel is in the camp of the combatants, and JHWH is
'with Israel'; and it must have already been like this for the
nucleus of the ones participating. The individual tribe is
precisely nothing but itself, but where an effective alliance
appears, be it only two or three tribes, there is 'Israel' " [56]—
not the amphictyony, but an Israel "for the concept of which
it is not essential how many of the tribes currently belonged
to it, but that it is undoubtedly a unity qualitatively distinct
from a sum total of tribes," [57] an Israel (thus one must add
by way of correction) which therefore in the Song of Deborah
is not called Israel.

From this perspective the significance of the Yahweh war
for the unity of Israel, already occasionally referred to above,
proceeds into a newer and sharper light. That Yahweh leads
the wars in itself gives them a pull toward the "expansion
into national status," [58] and we see this expansion in fact
even in the Song of Deborah as postulate and with Saul as
reality. Thus one may paraphrase what has been said up till
now: The war of Yahweh indeed is not derived from the
national status, but it leads to the national status. It does not
explain the quantum of the unity in the creation of the state

[55] v. Rad, *Der Heilige Krieg*, p. 26.
[56] Buber, *Königtum*, p. 127.
[57] *Ibid.*, p. 134.
[58] Alt, *Essays*, p. 192.

—for that, one must adhere to the tribal confederation as it was realized above; however, compelled by the urgency of the ever-increasing threat to expand to the neighbors, also by the leading of Yahweh and his agent capable of this expansion to include the neighbors as religious comrades and basically tending toward it, it is the most essential impulse leading to this unity.[59]

What was still semi-impotent "amphictyonic will" in the Song of Deborah becomes, in the formation of the state, reality: a politically negotiating union of the people within the territorial borders of the hitherto existing cultic, and as such politically powerless, twelve-tribe confederation.[60] The tradition attributes to Saul in the case of the summoning of the levy to the battle against the Ammonites an action which could be a variation of a custom which we encounter in connection with the procedure of the twelve-tribe confederation against the tribe of Benjamin.[61] Perhaps it is quite clear here how the new order supplants the old.[62] I Samuel 11 may or may not be historically reliable in the details; at any rate the event is symbolic for the change of the time. Henceforth those things which were hitherto antithetical, and only now and again approximated one another, are blended. Israel is hereafter a political entity[63]; the war of Yahweh, to be sure, does not turn into an institution, but its

[59] On the other hand, the enterprise of Abimelech (Judges 9), to which Professor D. O. Plöger draws my attention as a counterpart, had no future. Israelites and Canaanites have indeed lived together in Israel in a later stage of the formation of the state, but in a completely different way than it would have appeared with Abimelech, and only after the national unity of the Israelites had been established upon the above mentioned basis.

[60] The exact determination of the boundary is, as was already said, impossible. However, this is not the main point here, no more so than is the exact moment within the longer process of the establishment of the state.

[61] I Samuel 11:7; Judges 19:29-30; to that end G. Wallis, *ZAW*, 64 (1952) 57 ff.; however, also, M. Buber, *VT*, 6 (1959), 151.

[62] So Noth, *System*, p. 109-10; Alt, *Essays*, p. 193; G. Wallis, *ZAW*, 64:59.

[63] That the name could retain a different meaning or again acquire a new one is a matter in itself. Whether there still existed the cultic tribal confederation in the old or similar form after the establishing of the state cannot be said for certain.

leadership which suddenly originates with it and—at least according to the principle—just as suddenly again passes away, becomes an enduring kingdom.

That the twelve-tribe confederation, so to speak, shaped the channel in which the national political stream then flowed is, by the way, not so unnatural as one could surmise by an abstract dogmatizing of the dualism between Yahweh war and the tribal confederation. The only enduring association prior to the formation of the state had as yet to acquire through its existence in some way or other a meaning also in the political sense, not—it should be pointed out once more —because this was its intended purpose, but "inasmuch as a federation of twelve tribes in any case means an historical development of power, even when a deployment of power over against other powers does not belong to its essential tasks." [64] The Greek parallels thoroughly confirm this.[65]

Finally, if one once more evaluates the significance of the Yahweh war and of the tribal confederation for Yahweh and Israel over against each other and asks which of the two phenomena is the more "Yahwistic," there can scarcely exist any doubt that the distinction belongs to the Yahweh war. Unlike the tribal confederation, it is unthinkable without the god Yahweh, and it is often perceived as the noblest sphere of the confederation's activity.[66] A welcome illustration to that end is now furnished in the evidence of v. Rad,[67] that the "Day of Yahweh" originally means the war of Yahweh, hence not a cultic event, such as the postulated renewal festival of the confederation or else one of the annual festivals.

[64] Noth, *History,* p. 106

[65] Compare Cauer, *RE,* Vol. I, no. 2, columns 1920-21; Noth, *System,* p. 59. Here belongs the political role which the Ionic confederation played.

[66] Compare for example J. Wellhausen, *Israelitisch-jüdische Religion,* pp. 9-10; Hempel, *Gott und Mensch im Alten Testament,* p. 35; v. Rad, *Theology* I, 111 f. For a comparison with the amphictyony, v. Rad, *Studies in Deuteronomy* (1953), p. 45: "Perhaps it was here (the institution of the 'holy war') even more than in the Covenant Festival at Shechem that ancient Israel really first entered into her grand form."

[67] *Theology,* II, 119 ff.; also compare Wellhausen, *Geschichte,* p. 25.

3

Major and Minor Judges

In the first two chapters "the amphictyonic institution" was occasionally mentioned, and it was affirmed that it had nothing to do with the wars of Yahweh. As for "amphictyonic institution" some have up till now with serious reasons presumed above all two different things: a central sanctuary as was the case with the Greek amphictyonies, and the office of the "Judges of Israel."[1] It cannot be said emphatically enough that in this regard almost every detail is uncertain. Thus one must be exceedingly careful in drawing conclusions here and there from that which is incapable of proof, in arriving at new inferences from various conclusions of this kind, and in acquiring from that an image which the sources in their exceedingly fragmentary character simply do not yield. As already in the first two chapters, I shall try to compare that which is comparable—and in that respect the tradition surely offers something to our topic.

First of all, the office of the "Judge of Israel." The exegetical finding is well known.[2] In Judges 10:1-5; 12:7-15 six men are enumerated who, one after another, were sup-

---

[1] A further amphictyonic office is postulated by H. Graf Reventlow, *ThZ*, 15, (1959), 174-75: that of the מזכיר, whom he labels as the "public prosecutor of the confederation." Compare against that H. J. Boecker, *ThZ*, 17 (1961), 212 ff.

[2] Compare to the following M. Noth, *Festschrift für A. Bertholet* (1950), pp. 404 ff. The ingenious criticism of W. Richter (*ZAW*, 77 [1965], 40 ff.), in my opinion, labors especially in the crucial assertion of the dependence of the scheme of Judges upon the scheme of Kings (p. 46) with much too uncertain an argument to be able to conclusively disprove Noth's propositions.

posed to have "judged Israel" each for a certain number of years. For a long time no great significance was ascribed to this list, and it was thought to be a post-Deuteronomic product in which perhaps older material was used which can no longer be accounted for. However, Noth has dispelled the arguments for that and has made it plausible that it is a question of an old document of great historical value. Like the remaining previously doubted elements of the list, the name of Israel has also been placed in a new light. It would seem that it has to do with the twelve-tribe confederation. Apparently those six men, one after another, were the bearers of an office precisely in this confederation.[3] From the account of the dates, Noth[4] believes it can be concluded that people used these men for dating events. That would further emphasize the importance which this office must indeed have in our eyes because it appears to be the only total Israelite element about which the early tradition explicitly reports. It is highly noteworthy that judging by its name, it was not cultic. Here the parallel of the Greek amphictyony also breaks down.[5] On the basis of this parallel, the formula used concerning the sacred tribal confederation must at least be used *cum grano salis*. Not that the parallel for that reason is to be abandoned; it is now as before indispensable and will also render further positive service. But it is also important in the obvious variation, for in it there seems to be revealed a

[3] That would be valid independently of whether or not the area in which the word of these judges was acknowledged and obeyed was always exactly identical with that of the twelve tribes. Basically that was naturally the case, but actually there must have existed restrictions which may perhaps be equivalent to the list of tribes in the Song of Deborah. Compare also below, pp. 69-70.

[4] *Festschrift für A. Bertholet,* pp. 408, 414, n. 1.

[5] The corporate bodies of the pylaic-delphic amphictyony are composed of the representatives of the amphictyonies. Among several offices, for instance, is verified that of the director of the voting in the council of the Hieromnemons, only in the time of the Roman emperors that of a Ἑλλαδάρχης τῶν Ἀμφικτυόνων and that of a ἐπιμελητὴς τοῦ κοινοῦ τῶν Ἀμφικτυόνων (Cauer, *RE,* Vol. I, no. 2, columns 1924, 1927). The Etruscans elected annually a leader of the confederacy (v. Vacano, *Die Etrusker in der Welt der Antike* [1957], pp. 43-44).

peculiarity of Israel. In the twelve-tribe confederation the only function regularly performed through an office which we may presume, not only through inference and analogy but on the basis of explicit statements of the Old Testament, was a "judging." Its exact character is contested. With certainty it can only be said in the meantime that it is not a question of the normal jurisdiction; for that rested in the hands of the local communities.[6] The comparison with the Icelandic "proclaimers of law"[7] remains in some respects attractive, although it does not solve the difficulties of the exact definition of the Israelite office. If one should also assume here a proclamation of law according to the Icelandic analogy, then it remains open as to whether it concerns the utterance of casuistic or of apodictic laws or a combination of both as they are present before us particularly in the book of the covenant. One could cite grounds for each of these possibilities. But nevertheless the verb שפט points up an actual judging as the function of those figures and particularly so, since the proclamation of apodictic law, of which one might think first of all[8] according to what the Old Testament reports, seems to have been rather the concern of the Levites.[9] Proclamation of casuistic law, which rather would suggest itself according to the Icelandic parallel[10] as a function of the official speaker particularly of the Yahweh amphictyony, does not seem self-evident or obvious. Whether one may imagine the "judging" more exactly according to Deuteronomy 17:8, where the local jurisdiction for especially difficult cases is referred[11] to the central sanctuary and the Levitic priesthood there as well as "the judge who shall be

---

[6] Compare L. Köhler, *Hebrew Man* (1956), pp. 128 ff.

[7] Alt, *Essays*, pp. 102 ff.

[8] Compare Noth, *History*, p. 103.

[9] Compare esp. Alt, *Essays*, p. 125. H.-J. Kraus is concerned about the elimination of these difficulties in his *Die prophetische Verkündigung des Rechts in Israel* (1957).

[10] So Alt, *Essays*, pp. 102 ff.

[11] *Ibid.*, p. 103, n. 53.

there at that time," is dubious in view of the great distance in time between the old judge figures and Deuteronomy, even if of course some type of connection between the two categories of "Judges" is not excluded.[12] The important object את־ישׂראל which regularly follows וישׁפט in that old list rather points to facts which concern the confederation of tribes as such and its structure. Herein would fit particularly well the role of Joshua in Joshua 17:14 ff., to which Alt [13] refers: the acceptance of the grievance of the tribe of Joseph over too small an allotment of land. Joshua officiates here as a protector of the relationships between the tribes,[14] and that in an area to which, according to the Israelite view, belonged an exceptional sacred dignity. One may certainly question with G. v. Rad,[15] beginning with the conception of the character of the land as the gift of Yahweh to the people, if "that which Alt has taught us to understand under the concept of the 'territorial postulate of the tribes,' that is, those very old and in part very theoretical claims of certain tribes upon certain territories (should), not go back to the sacred ordinances which were fixed as binding from the center of the Yahweh amphictyony and from case to case." Here a שׁפט, with amphictyonic authority and in an amphictyonic framework, would be conceivable and necessary, and so Joshua 17:14 ff. may be considered as an example of the activity of the "Judge of Israel," although Joshua—whose traditionally historical connection with this pericope of Alt is regarded as especially stable[16]—does not appear in the list of the minor judges.[17]

[12] Compare above all Noth, *Festschrift Bertholet,* pp. 415-16.

[13] *Kleine Schriften,* II, 190-91.

[14] Joseph complains to Joshua "apparently in the expectation he would satisfy this demand at the expense of another tribe, thus through a new establishing of the borders to the advantage of Joseph" (Alt, p. 190).

[15] *Problem,* p. 86.

[16] Compare also M. Noth, *Das Buch Josua* (2nd ed., 1953), p. 106.

[17] It is possible that the list has not been completely passed on. Compare Noth, *Festschrift Bertholet,* pp. 414-15. Limits are set to the freedom of supplementation. H. W. Hertzberg, *Beiträge zur Traditionsgeschichte und Theologie des Alten Testaments* (1962), pp. 118 ff. adds on the strength of very different

Whichever of the mentioned activities the "Judges of Israel" may have exercised,[18] leadership in war was certainly not included.[19] The expression שפט, with which the list unfortunately only circumscribes their functions, denotes, according to internal and external Israelite parallels, civil administration and jurisdiction.[20] It was, of course, transferred by the Deuteronomic author of the Book of Judges to a number of war heroes whereby next to the true, but "minor," there appeared the figurative, but "major" judges.[21] Their action was by no means a "judging," and it relates to that of the real judges exactly as the war of Yahweh relates to the tribal confederation. What we have said above about the relationship of these two terms is confirmed in their most outstanding human exponents.

The contrast is obvious. Of some of them there is, except for the "judging," no historical action transmitted, only that this one had thirty sons upon thirty donkeys and they had thirty cities (Judges 10:4), that one, thirty sons and

---

arguments the names Othniel, Deborah, Abimelech, Gideon, Samuel, and Eli in order to complete the number twelve. The number twelve has been observed for a long time in the Book of Judges; compare, for example, H. Ewald, *Geschichte des Volkes Israel*, II (3rd ed., 1865), 513 ff.; Wellhausen, *Composition*, pp. 212-13. One took this number, to be sure, only as the imagination and postulate of the author or redactor of the Book of Judges and included in them, most likely in the sense of the latter, all judges present there (therefore, by Wellhausen and his followers the supposition that the minor judges were only added in order to complete a dozen). On the other hand, when one postulates a number twelve, esp. of the minor judges, one runs the risk of missing not only the intention of the Book of Judges (which can no longer distinguish between the two categories) but also the history (in which there hardly were exactly twelve).

[18] Naturally, combinations and changes are also possible. So could—the continuity between the old office of judge and that of Deuteronomy 17:9, 12 once presupposed—the fading away of the independence of the tribes after the creation of the state have brought about a shifting of the activity of the judge to that area described in Deuteronomy 17:8 ff.

[19] Strange to say, R. Kittel suspects among their number "tribal heroes who in the battles of conquest at different times, perhaps also several at the same time, have made themselves a name" (*Geschichte des Volkes Israel,* II [2nd ed., 1909], 80).

[20] Richter, *ZAW*, 77:57 ff.

[21] Compare above all Noth, *Überlieferungsgeschichtliche Studien,* pp. 47 ff.

thirty daughters and just as many sons-in-law and daughters-in-law from abroad (12:9), and a third one, forty sons and thirty grandsons upon seventy donkeys (12:14)—statistical curiosities which at least forcefully emphasize the lack of knowledge of historically important actions. On the other hand, there are the others! Here everything is action; without them we would know nothing about Barak or Gideon; only in this culminating point are they of consequence for the old tradition and therefore also visible for us. Jephthah sinks into the dark at that moment where he changes from a "major" to a "minor" judge. Now there is no longer anything to report about him, except for the "judging," the number of years, and the place of burial. The "minor" judges have indeed ultimately given their name to the "major," [22] but in other respects they have not been able to place their stamp upon the picture of that time. To be sure, the Deuteronomist has brought the entirely discontinuous sequence of the major judges into a continuity which in its very nature is contradictory throughout and has therewith to some extent also institutionalized it. However, his official regulations do not originate like the name from the minor judges, but are a schematization of what in his view constituted presupposi-

[22] It is superfluous to express conjectures as to what these could have been called earlier. Since H. Ewald, *Geschichte des Volkes Israel*, II (3rd ed., 1865), 509, n. 1, קָצִין has been preferred (compare esp. Judges 11:6, 11; Isaiah 3:6-7). An objection on the basis of the contents—that Jephthah, who was the only one to whom the expression was explicitly applied, was "no true charismatic" (compare Alt, *Essays*, p. 178, n. 14; v. Rad, *Der Heilige Krieg*, p. 27, n. 44)—would, in my opinion, not be valid. Jephthah was quite clearly declared to be a charismatic (see below). מוֹשִׁיעַ as proposed by Grether, *ZAW* 57 (1939), pp. 120-21, produces neither a very ancient impression nor that of a title; compare v. Rad, *Der Heilige Krieg*. Rather מגיד would come into consideration; compare R. Smend, *Die Bundesformel* (*Theol. Studien*, 68 [1963]), 19: W. Richter, *BZ* NF, 9 (1965), 71 ff. (certainly with discretion in relation to the concept of the charismatic leadership, p. 81, n. 40). Furthermore שפט is also not absolutely reliable as an old title of the minor judges. There appears in the list only from time to time וישפט; the participle appears in Judges 4:4 with verbal force; it appears as a title in Deuteronomic texts (Judges 2:16 ff.; II Samuel 7:11; II Kings 23:22; compare Ruth 1:1) to which one in this case cannot adhere. May one draw upon I Samuel 8:1*b* (see below p. 70)?

tions, issues and consequences of the appearance of the major judges. These determine the picture so completely and overwhelm the others so much that the less suspicious reader perceives them in their individuality just as little as he perceives the tribal confederation in contrast to the Yahweh war.

The major judges can be understood without the amphictyony. Their prerequisites lie somewhere else, namely above all in the peculiarity of the Israelite tribal situation. This hardly seems to have been any different from that of the clans (משפחות) just as the differentiation between these two types of associations in general seems to be difficult.[23] The tribe is evidently a less stable element than the clan and historically secondary to it, formed on the basis of certain situations, for instance, during and after the conquest of the land; consequently the tribe is, in the first place, a territorial power.[24] Obviously it is for the most part a community of interests, and here with the situation of the Israelites during their first time in the arable land, the military seems to predominate: the clans were not strong enough to resist the enemy from without (as was, perhaps, already the case in the conquest of the land or even in situations before that?) and for that reason banded themselves together in tribes.[25] The office of tribal chief is not attested to us and probably did not exist.[26] The "imbalance of the determining factors for the political formation of will and power, the aristocratic authority of the so-called elders on the one hand and the democratic institution of the assembly of all men of military capability on the other while they are without a monarchical leader"[27] demanded in occasional emergencies the leader-

[23] On this point above all J. Pedersen, *Israel*, I/II (1926), 29 ff.

[24] Compare B. Luther, *ZAW*, 21 (1901), 11; Noth, *System*, p. 78, n. 3; *History*, p. 106.

[25] Compare Luther, *ZAW*, 21: 14-15; A. Causse, *Du groupe éthnique à la communauté religieuse* (1937), pp. 17 ff.

[26] Compare finally R. de Vaux, *Das Alte Testament und seine Lebensordnungen*, I (1960), 34; differently, F. Horst, *RGG³* I (1957), column 335.

[27] Alt, *Essays*, p. 177.

ship of the confederation through an individual who func-
tioned for the time not by virtue of a permanent office.[28] Such
individuals were the major judges. Their "office" is not to
be understood "as a form of government . . . , but as a mandate to serve which was subject to and limited by the situation—an exclusively charismatic office whose interruptions
of occupancy thus ultimately belong to its nature." [29]

That these judges are persons who are "not supported
by an office, but by their role and the necessity of the circumstances," [30] does not say everything. Rather the "mandate to
serve" is added as a conclusive factor. If the war of Yahweh
were an event of the amphictyony, then this "mandate to
serve" must have ensued through its agents. This has actually
been asserted.[31] What does the tradition indicate?

The case most obvious to pragmatic thinking is that of
Jephthah. The Ammonites attack the land of Gilead. The
elders[32] of Gilead call upon their countryman Jephthah in
the land of Tob where he, expelled from his homeland, has
gathered "wanton men" around him and goes with them into
battle or on the prowl, and offer him the leadership in the
battle against the Ammonites and even beyond that—ob-

[28] According to R. Kittel, *Geschichte des Volkes Israel,* II (2nd ed., 1909),
103-4 in this case old Israelite-nomadic order from the time before the conquest of the land had once more come into force. Compare to this end also de
Vaux, *Des Alte Testament und seine Lebensordnungen,* I, 25-26. As to the
conditions of the contemporary Bedouin, M. Frh. v. Oppenheim, *Die Be-
duinen,* I (1939), 30-31; as for those of the old Arabs, J. Wellhausen,
Ein Gemeinwesen ohne Obrigkeit (1900), pp. 7-8.

[29] Buber, *Königtum,* p. 26.

[30] Wellhausen, *Prolegomena,* p. 127.

[31] Most strongly by H.-U. Nübel, *Davids Aufstieg in der Frühe israeliti-
scher Geschichtsschreibung* (Dissertation, Evangelical Theological Faculty,
Bonn, 1959), p. 140: "The judge of Israel had the right to designate the
commander of the army, and since the time of Saul, the king."

[32] So Judges 11:5-11. Previously (10:18), in addition to העם (see below),
mention is also made of שרי גלעד. The latter seems to be an addition; perhaps
verses 10, 17, and 18 also do not belong to the original history of 11:1 ff.,
compare Wellhausen, *Composition,* p. 223, n. 1; Täubler, *Biblische Studien,*
p. 281. If one considers it to be the "indispensable exposition of the entire
history," the alternative is to eliminate instead verse 11:4 (so Noth, *ZDPV,*
75 [1959], 35, n. 47). In support of the second possibility is the competition
of verse 4 with 5a.

viously to acquire his consent more readily. Jephthah agrees
to that, whereupon "the people" make him chief in war and
peace[33] over them. Parties to the agreement are very clearly
the people and the elders—thus the democratic and the aristocratic bodies, the second obviously only leading negotiations—from Gilead on one side, Jephthah on the other.
That the elders in an oath-like expression for the confirma-
tion of the contract[34] speak of Yahweh (11:10) and that
Jephthah represents the hoped-for victory in the usual lin-
guistic usage of the Yahweh war[35] as a delivering up of the
enemy to him through Yahweh (verse 9) and turns to Yahweh in prayer after the ensuing nomination by the people
(verse 11)[36] may not be interpreted in the sense that Yahweh
"is considered to be the real nominator."[37] Rather Yahweh
intervenes only at the beginning of the battle in such a way
that his spirit comes upon Jephthah (verse 29).[38] Where is
an amphictyonic commission to be found here?[39] There is
just as little of it to be seen in the behavior of the Gileadites
as in that of Yahweh. And Jephthah does not appear as
though he had already come as an emissary of the amphictyony to the afflicted Gileadites.[40] He was a minor judge, but
only after the Ammonite campaign. This sequence is important. Hence the judge of Israel does not lead the war of the
Gileadites against the Ammonites; on the contrary the one
approved in this local altercation, and then obviously also
as "leader of Gilead," ascends to the amphictyonic office.

[33] In the first attribute he is called קָצִין (11:6, 11), in the second רֹאשׁ
(10:18; 11:8, 9, 11).

[34] Compare Täubler, *Biblische Studien*, pp. 285-86.

[35] Compare v. Rad, *Der Heilige Krieg*, pp. 7-8.

[36] The "in Mizpah" at the end of the verse alludes, of course, to the sacred-
ness of the place; otherwise, no reference has been made to this.

[37] H. W. Hertzberg, *Die Bücher Josua, Richter, Ruth* (1954), p. 214.

[38] The secondary character of this verse and especially of its beginning
(compare finally Täubler, *Biblische Studien*, p. 286) is not provable; compare
Noth, *PJB*, 37 (1941), 71, n. 1; *ZDPV*, 75 (1959), 40, n. 55.

[39] The expression "Israelites" (as also in the insertion 11:12-28) on the
contrary does not come into use in 10:17.

[40] They turned to him because of his battle experience. According to
Täubler, *Biblische Studien*, p. 288, he was called with his band as its leader.

Gideon is somewhat less tangible for the historian. The appointment to the office of the leader ensues, according to the account in Judges 6:11 ff., not through the leading agents of the league of which Gideon was a member, but through Yahweh or his heralds. Later then, immediately prior to the military action, the spirit of Yahweh comes over Gideon (6:34) and only on the strength of that is the relationship of the leader to his warriors formed, this time at the initiative of the former (6:34b, 35). If we hold to this relation—an alternative cannot be derived with certainty from the indications in 8:17-18 which belong to an obviously independent tradition—it points up the common factor in the charismatic leadership between Gideon and Jephthah and therein that the subject of the appointment in both cases is clearly not an amphictyonic institution. Gideon however, unlike Jephthah, was not subsequently appointed to the amphictyonic office. The position which is offered to him in Judges 8:22 ff. can scarcely have been that of the Judge of Israel. If one wishes to make a comparison at this point with Jephthah, then the parallel lies rather with his position as "leader of Gilead." In both cases we would have to deal with the process of the continuation of the charismatic power through that which is enduring and institutional as Max Weber[41] has described it. This process necessarily has as content the continuation of the short-lived charismatic power in the same area, hence that of the political-military; otherwise one can scarcely conceive of the position of Jephthah as "head of Gilead" and the appointment of Gideon as "ruler of Israel." To that extent the non-political-military office of the Judge of Israel is not the direct continuation of the charismatic leadership, and it is not surprising that Jephthah is the only case where with certainty a major judge has become a minor one. That does not need to exclude the idea that it was the victory over the Ammonites which ensued with the help of the spirit of Yahweh, rather than the later continuous rule over Gilead, that predestined Jephthah for his amphictyonic office: he had shown himself therewith in closest association with Yahweh, who was also the God of the twelve-tribe confederation. But this spiritual state was temporary, being conferred only *ad hoc,* and so one also has to reckon with the possibility that Jephthah as the powerful representative of the league of Gilead administered the office of the Judge of Israel,[42] all the more so as we otherwise learn nothing of the previous charismatic actions of the Judges of Israel; but occasionally, even though in the form of an anecdote, we discover something of great wealth.

Of course, the tradition apart from the Book of Judges, and especially the list in Judges 10:1-5, 12:7-15, could suggest still another case where a charismatic leader had later exercised the functions of a Judge of Israel—that is, if Alt is correct with the thesis that Joshua was originally at home in the heroic legend of Joshua 10:1 ff., on the one hand, and in the traditions in Joshua 17:14 ff. and Joshua 24, on the other, and that the relationship therein is to be seen in such a way that "the authority which he (Joshua) as military leader had won first of all in the smaller circle, . . . could bring him the recognition as mediator of disputes between the tribes in a wider circle" and make him at the same time into the man "who placed Israel in the early epoch of its life in Palestine, through amalgamation around a new sanctuary of Yahweh in the heart of the land, upon the enduring foundation of its history." [43] Of course, no compelling proof can be produced for this view of the matter;[44] a certain inner probability, however, belongs to it. That Joshua does not

---

[42] Whether in conjunction with that of the "leader of Gilead" cannot be said.

[43] Alt, *Kleine Schriften,* II, 187 ff.

[44] The place of Joshua in the tradition of Joshua 10 is questioned by Noth, *Das Buch Josua,* p. 61; Noth rather considers it possible that Joshua has penetrated the legends of the conquest of the land in chapters 1-12 from his place in Joshua 24 (p. 139).

appear on the list of the minor judges indicates very little. The list does not have to be complete;[45] apart from this, the founder of the twelve-tribe confederation—and that Joshua seems to have been, according to Joshua 24—need not yet have been the bearer of an office which we find verified in later times in this confederation, and thus need not necessarily appear in the list. Perhaps the office was created after his death, so that these things which the founder had done (Joshua 17:14 ff.?)[46] could be continued in an institutional form. The amphictyonic function need not have been connected from the beginning with the office and his name. Be that as it may, it is not impossible that Joshua, the charismatic who later became "Judge," is a parallel to Jephthah; perhaps not only a parallel, but, by virtue of his outstanding position at the beginning, actually a conscious or unconscious example—to be sure, one that, as far as we can tell, was followed only once. This is not surprising, for the amphictyony surely did not always have at hand at each occurring vacancy of the office men who in war had been bearers of the spirit of Yahweh.[47] Unfortunately the figure of Joshua remains so obscure for us that we cannot say at all how far the parallel to Jephthah or to Gideon in particular could have reached. What we know about his call can by no means measure up in historical significance to the corresponding reports about Jephthah, indeed not even with those about Gideon. And so here, unfortunately, concerning both the temporal and material relationship between his function as leader in the war of Yahweh and as founder and—in order

[45] See n. 17 above. In my opinion one must reckon more seriously with the completeness of the list than is generally the case. That would imply that the office of the "Judge of Israel," for whatever reasons, did not necessarily exist the entire time between the conquest of the land and the creation of the state.

[46] May one also think of Joshua 24:25b?

[47] Of course, in the case of Joshua (as also in the case of Jephthah) the question remains open, whether by virtue of such a spiritual state or yet rather by virtue of a leading position in the tribe of Ephraim (or in the whole house of Joseph; perhaps also Benjamin as well?), he obtained the role in the twelve-tribe confederation.

to express it somewhat neutrally—*spiritus rector* in the twelve-tribe confederation, we do not have such ideal reference points as *mutatis mutandis,* in the case of Jephthah. But perhaps just the tradition of Jephthah as a clearer analogy provides a certain probability to Alt's thesis so that we may explain the inner logic of things here by analogy with those there.

In the instances thus far, no essential priority of the amphictyony over the war of Yahweh was to be discerned. The minor judges did not appear as leaders of war; in the case in which one man was both major and minor judge, the first attribute preceded the second. There exist, on the other hand, two cases which cannot be excluded in which a minor judge has appointed a major one. They certainly deserve serious consideration. But it must be said at the outset that even though that which has been said is not only not to be excluded but should be even likely or certain, these two cases should not or indeed do not have to determine the question as a whole. We have already seen in the first chapter that there were stages in the mutual approach of the war of Yahweh and the tribal confederation. It would not be surprising if we encountered them here again. Actually this is the case, for it concerns Deborah and Barak, and Samuel and Saul.

In the case of Deborah the absence from the list of minor judges is somewhat more serious than in the case of Joshua, insofar as incompleteness at the very beginning or at the very end (or both) is certainly to be assumed, presupposing that the office existed longer than the seventy-six years which the years of tenure in the list come to; but Deborah, unlike Joshua, will not have stood at the beginning or at the end. Nevertheless, there still remains a great deal of latitude. In any case, however, the absence from the list of Deborah just as in the case of Joshua means that a judgeship in the sense of the minor judges[48] cannot be proved, but is at best prob-

---

[48] F. Horst, *Gottes Recht* (1961), pp. 266-67 obviously thinks of a judgeship of a different kind.

able. It depends upon the strength of the positive indices. These are found in Judges 4:4 f.: "4*a* And Deborah, a prophetess, the wife of Lappidoth, 4*b* she judged Israel at that time. 5 And she dwelt under the palm tree (תמר) of Deborah between Ramah and Bethel in the hill country of Ephraim, and the Israelites came up to her for judgment." The verses are a good, even if not in this form, essential, exposition to what follows. 4*b* and 5 can be dispensed with and are often excluded as being secondary. It is to be urged above all that Deborah according to 5:15 seems to have belonged to Issachar, from which, oddly enough, the area between Ramah and Bethel lies far removed. Moreover, there existed "below Bethel," as denoted by אלון בכות, a tree under which according to Genesis 35:8 a different Deborah, the nurse of Rebekah, was buried. A secondary reference to the certainly more famous Deborah of the Song of Deborah suggests itself, and from this Judges 4:4*b*, 5 have often been declared to be historically worthless.[49] On the other hand תמר דבורה and אלון בכות are not necessarily the same. That at two localities which were not far from each other two different women were remembered with the same name, Deborah, is strange but not impossible. Once one accepts conditionally a historical basis of the report in Judges 4:4*b*, 5, then one difficulty which stands in the way of understanding the Song of Deborah[50] is diminished: one cannot properly perceive

[49] First, Wellhausen, *Composition*, p. 217; last, M. A. Beek, *Geschichte Israels* (1961), p. 38. R. Kittel at this point mutilates the sentence through omission of the words "between Ramah and Bethel in the hill country of Ephraim." According to H. Gressmann on this point there existed a palm tree of the Judge Deborah, but it stood "certainly in the region of Issachar." Ed. Meyer takes away from the tree the original reference to both Deborahs (*Die Israeliten und ihre Nachbarstämme* [1906], pp. 273, 277). G. Dalman, *JBL*, 48 (1929), 357 ff. differentiates between the palm of Deborah and the oak of lamentation. He seeks the first one in the region of el-bire; the second, which is located "below Bethel," does not fit this locality; thus the two are different.

[50] Not the one of Judges 4:6 ff. To that extent Budde is completely in the right at this point. But one may see fit to separate conditionally 4:4*b*, 5 as an unnecessary constituent of 4:4-24 and take it together with chap. 5 in the older and truer relation.

how the dimensions which extended far beyond the borders
of the restricted homeland of Barak (Naphtali, as well as its
neighbor Zebulun) and of Deborah (probably Issachar)
should have developed in which Israel participated in a battle
or in which its participation is at least later held to be fitting
in the Song. The participation of the tribes of middle Palestine can be explained by the influence of the woman dwelling in their midst and, according to the wording of our passage, endowed with high authority. But the reprimand in
the direction of the tribes living farther away who remained
apart from the battle would also become more understandable: if Deborah administered the office of the Judge of
Israel, then along with her participation in what happened,
she was given the position of keeping an eye on all the tribes,
of calling for assistance, of dispensing praise and reprimand.
This did not all have to be the personal work of Deborah; [51]
but perhaps here the weight of her office could be exerted
in a direction for which it was not intended but which was
forced upon it through the events—in view of the total
Israelite emergency, the only all-Israelite institution enters
into a kind of political action, not with apparent success in
terms of numbers and also with no more than a subsequent
reprimand against those who did not participate in the situation, but nevertheless with the result that there is also fortui-
tously the important postulate of a political-military unity
of the twelve-tribe confederation. One can, if need be, also
understand this result[52] without a judgeship of Deborah.
But it can hardly be denied that it would fit admirably in
the picture if in this situation the highest office of the amphictyony and the leadership of the war of Yahweh were
united in one person. The residence of Deborah between
Ramah and Bethel, which is often brought to bear against
the trustworthiness of Judges 4:4b, 5, speaks, when one does

[51] Perhaps also in the sense that she had composed the song attributed to
her.

[52] Compare Chap. I above.

not believe in a confusion of the two Deborahs and the
identity of their trees, from a perspective for, rather than
against, the passage. We know of yet another Judge of Israel
who came from Issachar, namely Tola.[53] His place of resi-
dency and action according to Judges 10:1 lay not in the
region of his native tribe, but "he lived in Shamir in the hill
country of Ephraim." That corresponds entirely to "she dwelt
under the palm tree of Deborah between Ramah and Bethel
in the hill country of Ephraim" in Judges 4:5. Here as there,
a descendant of Issachar performed a judicial function in the
hill country of Ephraim. The state of affairs is thus, in any
case, not unique, and therefore in the case of Deborah can
at least be considered as possible. Apparently the conditions
for the judicial function were more favorable in the hill
country of Ephraim than in Issachar. In the first place perhaps for geographical reasons: as demonstrated by the build-
ing of the capitals in the time of Kings, and also by the conditions already in the amphictyony, so far as they are still
known to us,[54] the hill country of Ephraim is the natural
center of the land. Unfortunately we are not informed about
the place of activity of all the Judges of Israel; indeed, we are
informed precisely only in the case of Tola.[55] As for the
others, besides the origin, only the burial place is stated,
which (except for Tola) evidently always lies in the original homeland.[56] For that reason one cannot exclude the possi-

---

[53] Regarding him, compare Noth, *Festschrift Bertholet* (1950), pp. 409-10.
The explanation of the circumstances given in the following seems to me
less applicable than the conclusion often drawn from it of a secondary
migration of Issachar from the hill country of Ephraim (for example, Alt,
Kleine Schriften, I, 126, n. 4). In addition to this, also Noth, *History,* p. 78,
n. 1.

[54] On this point, compare the next chapter.

[55] Moreover (apart from Deborah) in the case of Samuel, if he was a
judge; on that point, see further below. As for the doubtful case of Elon,
compare Noth, *Festschrift Bertholet,* pp. 411-12; Hertzberg, *Beiträge zur
Traditionsgeschichte und Theologie des Alten Testaments* (1962), p. 124.
Hertzberg suspects that the case of Elon is similar to that of Deborah and
Tola.

[56] In the case of Jair we cannot say because we do not know where Kamon
(Judges 10:5) was located; compare Noth, *Festscrift Bertholet,* p. 410, n. 2.

bility, indeed not even hold it unlikely, that the judges in the execution of their offices did not go out from their homeland into the center of the land or even take up residence elsewhere.[57] Accordingly the geographical reasons are hardly sufficient to explain the special circumstances in the case of Tola (and Deborah). But besides, or in place of that, one may perhaps refer to the political situation of the tribe of Issachar, as Alt[58] has concluded from Genesis 49:14-15 in combination with the Amarna letter A07098: a settlement in the territory of Sunem with recognition of Canaanite supremacy; freedom for the first time finally in the time of David. In this situation apparently membership of the tribe in the amphictyony—especially considering its nonpolitical character—is certainly possible, but the proper place for the official seat of the Judge of Israel is certainly not here. Thus Tola officiates away from home. The case can be directly applied to Deborah. Her personal intervention in the battle against the Canaanites was especially for the benefit of her own tribe Issachar. From this point of view it is not inconceivable that the union of tribal confederation and Yahweh war precisely in the person of Deborah was no accident. The endeavor at this point to know more would of course lead into the area of speculation. In general, the judgeship of Deborah is only a possibility, even after what has been said, indeed a thoroughly debatable one.

If one decides in this sense for the historicity of Judges 4:4b, 5, then to be sure the problem of the entire fourth chapter of Judges placed before us in our context is not yet solved. As the incident is described there, Deborah in the name of Yahweh orders Barak to the battle against Sisera. In what capacity does she do this? As Judge of Israel? That

---

For a conjecture as to why the gravesite used to be mentioned, see Nübel, *Davids Aufstieg*, p. 125, n. 110.

[57] Any residence in the central sanctuary at all, according to Judges 10:1, is out of the question.

[58] *Kleine Schriften*, III, 174-75.

would be extremely peculiar, so much the more since in verse 4a the title נביאה is also attributed to her. If one holds to this, then the event takes its place in the series of calls of political-military leaders through the prophets which are reported to us in the Old Testament. Presumably the narrator has regarded it as such, and in fact it becomes more intelligible in that way. But then it also loses historical probability to the extent that one assumes a critical stance with regard to the existence of a prophet at such an early time. One may imagine Deborah as a seeress who anticipated the functions of later prophets; or one may suppose that the title נביאה was conferred upon her by virtue of a function other than the later familiar prophetic one[59] and that it then, in another connotation, attracted to itself the story of the call. Be that as it may, in any case the nature of the participation of Deborah in the occurrences can no longer be precisely clarified.[60] Indeed some have even reversed the relationship between her warlike and her judicial activity and supposed that the note 4:4b, 5 belongs at the end of the story, "because it refers to the time after the Taanach victory and to the authority which Deborah acquired through it."[61] Deborah then would belong close together with Jephthah[62] and would fall less out of order than is now the case. In principle something can be said for this, and it would naturally prove more directly useful to the main thesis of the present work than the temporal priority of the office of the judge. However,

---

[59] On this point, compare A. Jepsen, *Nabi* (1934), p. 236.

[60] Following Wellhausen, *Composition*, p. 217: "according to 5:12 where Luther surely translates correctly 'capture your captors' and the punctuation vocalizes only for harmonistic reasons 'capture your captives,' Barak seems to have had a personal motive against the Canaanites and to have obeyed the summons of Deborah without hesitation." This passage should be placed by the side of Judges 8:18-19. An appointment of Barak, thus of one especially affected by the political situation, through Deborah would then be possible and even significant.

[61] Buber, *Königtum*, p. 142.

[62] *Ibid.*: "at the beginning was probably reported, as in other stories of Judges, the seizure by the spirit—a report which for some unknown reason was then lost."

according to what was developed above and in Chapter I, even the latter does not stand in the way of the thesis and I would prefer it as over against the assumption of Buber.

The figure of Samuel puts the historian in an even greater dilemma than that of Deborah. Here he has more sources than there; but this is only apparently an advantage. None of the authenticity which the Song of Deborah in all its obscurity possesses is present, and the picture which the sources produce as a whole is contradictory and scarcely shows the historical Samuel; one must decide upon one or the other, but even then one does not have the assurance of standing on firm ground. Moreover, doubly important for our problem is that the historical situation in which Samuel appeared, even more so than with Deborah, was a crisis. The situation given there appears not only like the case of Deborah, one where "the national and religious emergency has allowed for a 'judge' figure[63] to rise above the routine functions of the office" and where one consequently does not succeed with a purely institutional description "because this criterion is not sufficient for the comprehension of the great figures of the Old Testament" [64]—but therein lies precisely an advantage in that one can see by this criterion what person, charisma, and situation have added to the institutional. In the case of Samuel, in addition to what has been said, it is a question of the situation of a radical change which one can hardly overrate: the creation of a state. In what respect does Samuel stand on this side; in what respect on the other side? To what extent is he, perhaps, originator of the radical change and at the same time or later also its mourner, or, on the other hand, the symbolic figure about whom the conceptions of the historical circumstances have solidified? It is painful for our investigation that these questions can only be answered quite vaguely. If we knew more

[63] Once it is assumed that it is such a question in both instances.

[64] A. Weiser, *Samuel, Seine geschichtliche Aufgabe und religiöse Bedeutung* (*FRLANT*, 81 [1962], 16).

about Samuel, we could perhaps, inferring from him, say much more about the time prior to the formation of the state than is now possible for us. Under these circumstances it would almost mean trying to explain an *ignotum ab ignoto* if we were to make him into the central figure of a working hypothesis, somewhat in the sense that one would suppose Samuel, as the bearer of the office of the Judge of Israel, appointed Saul to be leader of the levy and then inferred from that that the Judge of Israel generally by virtue of his office possessed the right to such an act. For the aforementioned supposition, as we shall see, the basis in the sources is not firm enough; for the generalizing conclusion, the situation is too extraordinary. What can be offered here under such presuppositions is not the apparently hopeless attempt to clear up the "Samuel-Saul literary complex," but only some few aspects which touch upon our line of inquiry.

Among the accounts which deal with Saul's becoming king, scholarship usually ascribes the greatest value to that in I Samuel 11.[65] According to general consensus it is at least doubtful as to whether or not Samuel is originally mentioned in it at all.[66] "The entire people" or "all the men of Israel" (verse 15) are the ones who here in a holy place in Gilgal "make" Saul "King." It is a question of what has been called the "democratic principle" of the Israelite monarchy[67] and of what later confronts us as such in similar form again and again, the installation of the king through acclamation of the

[65] According to Buber, *VT*, 6 (1956), it is the only one for which "a source in the literary sense" can be assumed. A deciding factor for its historicity is the subsequent devotion of the inhabitants of Jabesh-gilead to Saul and his family (I Samuel 31:11 ff.; II Samuel 2:4 ff.; 21:11 ff.). Compare G. Hölscher, *Geschichtsschreibung in Israel* (1952), p. 92. That it is simply a question in I Samuel 11 of a "historical narrative" in contrast to the "legend" in Chap. 9 (Gressmann, *Die Schriften des Alten Testaments*, Vol. II, no. 1 [2nd ed., 1921], p. 43), seems to me indeed exaggerated.

[66] The words ואחר שמואל (verse 7) are probably trustworthy; verses 12-14 are likely an addition. The introduction of Samuel in verse 15 by the LXX is secondary.

[67] J. A. Soggin, *ThZ*, 15 (1959), 403 ff.

people[68] and no doubt as a rule on the basis of an "alliance" between king and people.[69] Similarly "the people" (of Gilead) had once made Jephthah their leader (Judges 11: 11); and according to the tradition in Judges 8:22, "the men of Israel" had taken a step toward such action on behalf of all Israel when they offered the monarchy to Gideon. According to verse 23 Gideon was deterred from that, which is proof of the fact that "in Israel certain inhibitions against a further development in this direction" must have existed.[70] But the development which led to the point at which Israel constituted itself in a political sense as "nation" could not be delayed for long. Gilead (in the above example) had perhaps already reached that stage, but Israel as a whole in any event only reached it in the short flare-up wherein the tribal confederation and the war of Yahweh had entered upon the closest connection with each other up until that time, and where the Song of Deborah had avowed, at least indirectly, the necessity of the identity between Israel and the people (of Yahweh).[71] The event in I Samuel 11:15 was now truly and ultimately "a political act." Israel here no longer acted as a sacred tribal confederation, but as a "nation." Here Israel entered upon the road to a political power structure, even if at first only in a quite modest manner, and in so doing implemented a decision which essentially determined the further course of its history.[72] The amphictyony constituted itself as a political corporation and thereby relinquished its amphictyonic character.

The acclamation by which Saul was made king certainly did not occur without preparation. On the contrary, it was doubtless a question of the culmination of a process in which the necessity of the kingdom in general and the qualification of Saul in particular had to be proved. As far as the first

---

[68] Compare Alt, *Essays*, p. 191, and elsewhere.
[69] Compare G. Fohrer, *ZAW*, 71 (1959), 1 ff.
[70] Noth, *History*, p. 163.
[71] See above, pp. 13-14.
[72] Noth, *History*, p. 171.

point is concerned, the creation of the Israelite state was a result of the threat by the Philistines.[73] Strange to say, this motif does not appear at all in I Samuel 11. That does not mean, however, that it could not have been in the background here, and that according to the view of this narrator, Saul was not being made king with regard to the Philistine war. Thus it does not speak against the historical character of I Samuel 11. For the question to which the chapter replies is not why a king was necessary at that time, but how Saul became this king. This is precisely as it was in the case of Gideon: the one upon whom the spirit of Yahweh had come in the battle is the candidate for the permanent ruling position. "I [Samuel] 11 has shown that in Saul a highly gifted improviser of the holy war had been discovered. The old tradition required a new one for each war"[74]—the chronic military necessity demands constant leadership of which one may speak to begin with as an extended judgeship rather than a thoroughgoing kingdom,[75] but with which the hitherto existing order is abandoned so radically that formulations such as that the king is "originally the military leader of the twelve tribe confederation," "so to speak an official of the Yahweh amphictyony,"[76] can hardly be appropriate.

The authority for Saul's kingship is his charisma in the Ammonite battle. But is that sufficient? To keep with the examples already repeatedly referred to: the spirit comes over Gideon after he is called upon by Yahweh, over Jephthah after he is made leader by the Gileadites, over both (as over Saul) only immediately before the decisive battle. Complete authority for the continuing office does not, therefore, seem to lie in the resulting spiritually inspired victory in the war of Yahweh. Does this also apply to Saul, so that what has

---

[73] Compare above all, Alt, *Essays,* pp. 173 ff., 197.

[74] W. Caspari, *Die Samuelbücher* (1926) , p. 122.

[75] Soggin, *ThZ,* 15: 411. Differently now, W. Beyerlin, *ZAW,* 73 (1961) , 186 ff.; Weiser, *Samuel,* p. 54.

[76] H. Wildberger, *ThZ,* 13 (1957) , 468.

been told in I Samuel 11 must necessarily be preceded by something of that kind? On the basis of I Samuel 11 it is difficult to say; indeed, one is inclined toward a No. The threatened Gileadites (unlike their ancestors once did, Judges 11) do not turn toward a definite man already familiar to them who should assume the leadership of their army; but they send out messengers apparently indiscriminately "into all the territory of Israel" in the hope that there is someone who "will deliver" them (verse 3). The choice falls upon Saul only indirectly—the narrative obviously wishes to exclude with care the idea that he had already been chosen as far as the people were concerned, and with that to underscore the apparent fortuitousness, the real wonder of the event. When the messengers from Jabesh arrive in Gilead, Saul is not even there; he comes later from the field, sees the people weeping, and inquires as to the reason. Only then does he learn about the matter, not from the messengers but from the people.[77] Instantly the spirit of God seizes him and he summons the army to battle. This in itself is an intelligible and complete account; it "produces an unbroken and very profound impression, even if Saul himself had no idea of his national destiny." [78] Can one from this perspective disregard the preceding? According to Caspari,[79] "later opinion," referring to I Samuel 11, finds "a gap in his (Saul's) development. That the spirit which is crucial for his appearance overpowers him unannounced with signal success could, although restricted to the time before the kings, nevertheless be exploited as a carte blanche for any violent political revolution by unauthorized persons who simply presume for themselves authority over their countrymen. Therefore the unexpected-

---

[77] One could only be disconcerted that Saul, according to verse 7, sends out *"the messengers"* (LXX^B omits the article). They are evidently those from Gilead who are then to be thought of as the ones that remained in Gibeah. Yet it would be hair-splitting to want to conclude from that, that they had waited for Saul to return home.

[78] Caspari, *Die Samuelbücher*, p. 122.

[79] *Ibid.*, pp. 122-23.

ness of the appearance of the spirit should be left solely to public participation. The bearer of the spirit must be able to prove himself believable with regard to his qualification, independent of his success; he must also be able to bring forward a witness who dispels every suspicion of an error in the preliminary procedures; the bestowal of spirit presupposes a rite. All this I Samuel 9 ff. achieves as the substructure for I Samuel 11." The argumentation is quite clear, and I can see no way to refute it. If it proves correct, then Samuel is eliminated from direct participation in Saul's becoming king. In reality that always remains possible, if not probable. On the other hand it can be asserted against the demonstrated judgment of I Samuel 11 that the chapter with the preceeding is now interwoven into—one can hardly express it any other way—a wonderful unity.[80] Certainly in chapter 11 Saul acts "as though nothing had happened."[81] But—in spite of Caspari—what would the narrative be for the reader today without the previous encounter of Saul with Samuel? Its charm now lies precisely in how the paths of the unsuspecting messengers from Gilead and the one designated by Yahweh are brought together through divine providence. The concealment and secrecy of the one nominated between nomination and public appearance is a genuine biblical motif which could have been misconstrued by the editors and redactors[82] but which nevertheless originates from actuality. Even if this is historically still scarcely comprehensible, one cannot quite exclude the possibility that behind chapters 8-10 also lie historical events. From these one could hardly imagine Samuel as absent, in contrast to the Ammonite war and Saul's becoming king following it.

Of the two versions which confront each other here, the one in 8; 10:17-27a according to the text has greater ideologi-

---

[80] Compare on this point esp. M. Buber, *VT*, 6 (1956), 122-23 and elsewhere.

[81] *Ibid.*, p. 147.

[82] Compare on this point also p. 126 below.

cal testimonial content and claim. But temporally it is far away from the events, and materially, is a product of late reflection about the kingdom as a whole.[83] Moreover, it does not stand to I Samuel 11 in the relation of a possible supplement but rather in that of opposition. That before the Ammonite war Saul is already the secret king, anointed by Samuel but not even known as such to his own uncle, can be imagined.[84] On the other hand, that the entire national assembly already deliberates in detail concerning the king, indeed has already ascertained him through the lot,[85] is insupportable prior to Chapter 11. Thus one may understand 8; 10:17 ff. as an "elaborate, expanded parallel to 11:15" [86] or even speak of that in 11:15 as "told identically with what is reported in 10:21b-27" [87]—the concise statement in 11:15 remains the only one which is credibly expressed concerning the "democratic principle" in the case of Saul's becoming king.[88] So we no longer need to be occupied with the necessity [89] and function of the figure of Samuel here in 8; 10:17 ff.

According to age, and perhaps also[90] to the historical value, 9:1–10:16 is more important. Certainly it is a question

[83] That is not altered by the fact that one tries to establish the historical possibility of some of its motives already for the time at the threshold of the creation of the state, as has been tried most recently in various ways by Buber, *In memoriam Ernst Lohmeyer* (1951), pp. 53 ff. and Weiser, *Samuel*, pp. 32 ff.

[84] Thus, the literary critical school has been able to take I Samuel 9:1–10:16 as a natural unity with Chap. 11; compare Wellhausen, *Composition*, pp. 242-43.

[85] Buber certainly excludes this latter feature, *VT*, 6: 142-43.

[86] Soggin, *ThZ*, 15:407.

[87] Wildberger, *ThZ*, 13: 468; compare also R. Press, *Theologische Blätter*, Vol. 12 (1933) , columns 247-48; *ZAW*, 56 (1938) , 204-5.

[88] Also, a missing report perhaps between 11:11 and 15 as to how (under the presupposition of 9:1–10:16) "precisely through Samuel's suggestion the people should have hit upon the idea of making their savior now also king" (J. Wellhausen, *Der Text der Bücher Samuelis* [1871], p. 77) , or how (independent of 9:1–10:16) "Saul was called by Samuel to be king" (Wildberger, *ThZ*, 13:468) cannot be reconstructed from any component of 8; 10:17 ff.

[89] Contested by Soggin, *ThZ*, 15: 406. Compare on this problem primarily Caspari, *Die Samuelbücher*, pp. 82, 116 (on 10:17) .

[90] Despite the negative judgment of K. Möhlenbrink, *ZAW*, 58 (1940/41) , 66, n. 2.

of tradition; indeed, one may speak of legend in some instances.[91] But as "substructure" for Chapter 11, the passage
no doubt has an early existence there; as such, of course,
it is also extremely difficult to scrutinize. Subsequently it is
told (by Saul himself?) in order to establish the authority of
his kingdom; in spite of the remarkable assembly at the place
of sacrifice in Ramah,[92] in the crucial moment, without wit-
nesses, secret, the event evades our grasp. But we can hardly
learn in a more original form than here of the relation between Samuel and Saul, if it existed at all [93] and beyond that
was not merely an unofficial, personal "friendship." [94] The
situation, without question, is one which we know otherwise
as that of the call of a king through a prophet in the course
of which especially the anointing can have its place (compare
especially I Kings 11:29 ff.; 19:15-16; II Kings 9:1 ff.).[95]
Accordingly Samuel's behavior toward Saul hardly differs
from the function of later prophets,[96] and to that extent the

[91] Buber, *Königtum*, p. 142: "a hybrid of legend and fairy tale"; Noth,
Überlieferungsgeschichtliche Studien, p. 24, n. 5: "idyllic folktale"; G.
Hölscher, *Geschichtsschreibung in Israel* (1952), p. 91: "a poetic work in the
style of the happy fairy tale"; Weiser, *Samuel*, p. 48: "legend woven through
with fairy tale motifs."

[92] Some readily ascribe to it an "atmosphere of conspiracy"; most recently
Wildberger, *ThZ*, 13: 454. According to some, it is the Assembly of elders of
Israel which met there, and to which Samuel thus presents the future king
and which is thus participating in his call; in this esp. Buber, *In memoriam
E. Lohmeyer*, p. 65; *VT*, 6: 129-30 (with an interesting parallel from Sparta,
141; Wildberger, *ThZ*, 13: 465; opposed to that, G. Fohrer, *ZAW*, 71 (1959),
3, n. 8; Weiser, *Samuel*, p. 51, n. 8.

[93] "That the various traditions despite their variety are in agreement at
this point" (Weiser, *Samuel*, p. 26) is no compelling proof for it; I Samuel
9:1–10:16 can be fiction and everything else developed from that. Also, compare however, Soggin, *ThZ*, 15: 412.

[94] Compare Gressmann, *Die Schriften des Alten Testaments*, Vol. II, no.
1, p. 36.

[95] Anointing by the prophets is certainly not attested early; David is
anointed by the men of Judah to be King of Judah (II Samuel 2:4), by the
elders of Israel to be King of Israel (II Samuel 5:3); compare also II
Kings 11:12. The participation of Nathan at the anointing of Solomon (I
Kings 1:34, 45) is questionable (verse 39!). Naturally, I Samuel 16:1-13 is
completely excluded as evidence for the early period.

[96] Whether one can call him a prophet in the later sense of the word on
the basis of this (compare above all, R. Press, *ZAW*, 56 [1938], 177 ff.) is a
different question, likely to be answered negatively.

expressions "man of God" (9:6 ff., compare I Kings 17:18, 24; II Kings 1:9 ff. for Elijah; II Kings 4:7 and other passages for Elisha) and "seer" (9:9, 11, 12; in verse 9 the famous equation with the later "prophet") agree. Our narrative perceives the event in this manner, and we cannot get behind it, not even through an elimination of parts of the text which contain these expressions.[97] As previously the "prophetess" Deborah in the name of Yahweh summoned Barak to the battle, so the "prophet" Samuel in the name of Yahweh anoints Saul to be King.[98] This is the statement of the text. The supposition that "according to what is then imparted in I Samuel 11" it must "at least appear to be doubtful, if by the call of Saul one was already thinking of a future kingship and not merely, to begin with, of leadership during momentary distress," so that perhaps Samuel had only "inspired Saul at his first appearance," [99] has no basis.

But just as unlikely is the thesis that Samuel in his role as "Judge of Israel" has appointed Saul and anointed him.[100]

That he was endowed with this attribute is to be sure quite possible, just as in the case of Deborah. In I Samuel 7:15-17a it is reported: "15 And Samuel judged Israel all the days of his life. 16 And he went from year to year in circuit to Bethel, Gilgal and Mizpah and judged Israel at all these places. 17a And he returned to Ramah for there was his house and there he judged Israel." The last sentence sounds somewhat awkward; Ramah may stem from I Samuel 1:19; 2:11.[101] However, the names of places in verse 16 appear not

---

[97] Wildberger's separation into one "kernel" (9:22–10:1, 3, 4) and diverse "legendary description" (*ThZ*, 13: 452 ff.) distorts the sense of the narrative.

[98] Or to be the נגיד.

[99] Noth, *History*, pp. 169-70. The reference there to I Samuel 11 would have more weight if 9:1–10:16 and 11 were not contrasted so clearly against each other as two incidents. The Ammonite victory is an event in itself which is supposed to manifest Saul as a charismatic and provoke the acclamation of the people. The anointing story aims at more than that. Compare now Beyerlin, *ZAW*, Vol. 73.

[100] So Wildberger, *ThZ*, 13: 463 ff.

[101] So Noth, *Überlieferungsgeschichtliche Studien*, p. 56, n. 6; opposed to that, Weiser, *Samuel*, p. 10, n. 1.

to be contrived and could be an old tradition.[102] In addition, there is the statement about the judgeship of his sons in Beer-sheba (8:1-2) which belongs together with the preceding as a "chronicle-like note";[103] now, to be sure, it must serve, moreover, to introduce the not necessarily ancient[104] motif of their disobedience (verse 3), which for its part is supposed to motivate verses 4 ff. The statement can be thoroughly comprehended; even if not, or not only, for the reasons of age declared in verse 1 (the office was, of course, for life), then at least perhaps, or perhaps also, for geographical reasons: difficulties in the administration of justice from the center of the region for the isolated south, relief through the installation of judges on the spot.[105] Thus one may ascribe some value to the report of the judging by the sons[106] and also in that way[107] find the acceptance of the judgship of the father sustained, which in the last few years with more or less great confidence has been more frequently advocated.[108] If that is correct, then the essential disparity of the Samuel legends with the history is doubly regrettable; for under these circumstances our already exceedingly scanty knowledge of the functions of the Judge of Israel, despite the great deal which we apparently know of Samuel, is not enlarged in any way.[109] Also, the early history of his judgeship is unknown. Some readily speak of his connections with Shiloh as the

[102] Noth, *Überlieferungsgeschichtliche Studien.*

[103] Buber, *In memoriam E. Lohmeyer,* p. 55, n. 8.

[104] It strongly suggests I Samuel 2:12 ff., but is paler and motivates what follows unsatisfactorily.

[105] Or did only one reside in Beer-sheba, the other in Bethel? So Josephus, *Antiquities,* Vol. VI, no. 3, p. 2.

[106] With Noth, *Überlieferungsgeschichtliche Studien,* p. 56, n. 7.

[107] Certainly less through the parallel which Weiser, *Samuel,* p. 29, n. 1, draws to the entirely different anecdote-like statements in Judges 10:3-4; 12:8-9, 13-14.

[108] H. W. Hertzberg, *Beiträge zur Traditionsgeschichte und Theologie des Alten Testaments* (1962), p. 121; v. Rad, *Theology,* I, 58-59, and II, 7, n. 2; Noth, *Laws,* p. 244, n. 37; Weiser, *Samuel,* pp. 10-11.

[109] All kinds of suppositions on the basis of recent texts by Weiser, *Samuel,* pp. 11 ff., 83 ff.

amphictyonic central sanctuary;[110] but the historian can scarcely attach any value to the early history of I Samuel 1 ff., and it is doubtful if Shiloh was the central sanctuary.[111] Was his course similar to that of Jephthah, from major to minor judge? In I Samuel 7 he appears only as one praying.[112] That could be the blurring of more original evidence in the sense of the transformation of the conceptions of the war of Yahweh, but the original evidence does not shine through, and 12:2 where Samuel is drawn up with Jerubbaal, Barak, and Jephthah is Deuteronomic. Does the conception as prophet in the story of Saul's anointing and at other times[113] give an indication? It could then be considered a similar combination as in the case of Deborah. But the case there, as we have seen, does not have quite the soundness which would be necessary in order to make feasible a conclusion from analogy; and anointing by a prophet, as well as the prophethood itself, are questionable in the period prior to the formation of the state. The relationship between judge and prophet which Wildberger[114] sees grounded in that both "had their spiritual home in the traditions of the old Yahweh amphictyony," both were "fighters for the law of God," is abstract.

After all that, a "complete picture" [115] seems to me to be remote. Some kind of relationship may have existed between Samuel and Saul; and the extent of Saul's leadership and kingdom in Israel as a whole may be deduced from that, although in I Samuel 11:7 Saul does act on his own responsibility. Even a designation of the leader and king by the judge could have taken place and could have been understood

---

[110] Compare E. Auerbach, *Wüste und Gelobtes Land,* I (1932), 172; H.-J. Kraus, *Prophet und Politik* (1952), p. 37.

[111] See Chap. IV below.

[112] Buber, *Der Glaube der Propheten* (1950), p. 97; *VT,* 6: 119; Weiser, *Samuel,* pp. 17, 21.

[113] Compare Press, *ZAW,* 56: 177 ff. and Buber, *VT,* 6: 125-26, 162, 168-69, and elsewhere.

[114] *ThZ,* 13: 464-65.

[115] *Ibid.,* p. 468.

only by later writers as anointing by the prophet and could
have been replaced by it. We know nothing about that, and
if it were the case, we could learn little from it about the
old amphictyony. For it is no longer a question of the old
"summoning to mission conditioned and limited by the situation," but of the establishing of a new office, indeed an office
after all at a point where up until now there was only the
charisma. If in this act the "men of Israel" take the step
from amphictyony to people and state, then the "Judge of
Israel" does not stay within his previous limitations, assum-
ing that he participates in the act. One would be able to draw
no conclusions from his participation for the past. If one
wishes to establish this alternative, the kingdom stands nearer
to the charismatic leadership than to the amphictyony;[116] but
it is something new, a third entity over against the other two.

I will now summarize. The most outstanding human
representatives of Yahweh war and tribal confederation are
in later tradition called by the same name. This name, however, rightly belongs only to the officials of the tribal confederation; the secondary transference to the charismatic
leaders of the Yahweh war is further evidence for the fact that
after centuries one no longer recognized the old dualism and
viewed the time prior to the formation of the state as more
uniform than it had been in reality. A combining in one
person of the two "offices" (of which, indeed, only one is
really an office) is not verified. Where a single individual
did perform both, it took place successively and in such a
way that the charismatic deed preceded the amphictyonic
office (Jephthah). In the two cases in which bearers of the
amphictyonic office seem to participate in the war of Yahweh (Deborah, Samuel), it is uncertain in both instances as
to whether it concerns actual "judges"; furthermore the
summoning to mission which is issued through them in both
instances does not appear in the oldest layer of the tradition;

---

[116] Alt, *Essays,* pp. 190 ff.; conversely, Wildberger, *ThZ,* 13: 468, n. 60.

finally, the situation in both instances is so extraordinary that exceptions to the rule, or the step from the old and normal to something new, would be possible and probable. The conclusion of the first two chapters finds corroboration through all that.

That is even true of the last sentences of the second chapter, which spoke of the close relation of Yahweh to the "holy war." This relation takes shape particularly in that the spirit of Yahweh comes over the leader; hence Yahweh himself actually acts in him.[117] That is not told of all great warriors of the time of Judges, for there were at that time, besides the wars of Yahweh, also other battles[118] and leaders[119] whom one may, of course, in the broader sense of the word[120] call charismatics, but not in the stricter sense which entails that the charisma operating in the respective leader is the spirit of Yahweh himself and is even so identified. Some have wanted to exclude Judges 6:34, 11:29 and I Samuel 11:6 from the original narratives.[121] Actually the expression is also found in late passages,[122] but that is not sufficient to deem those referred to as late.[123] At the worst they would

---

[117] This is nicely expressed apart from the testimony of the spirit also in the war cry "The sword for Yahweh and for Gideon" (Judges 7:20); compare Buber, *Der Glaube der Propheten* (1950), p. 90.

[118] Compare v. Rad, *Der Heilige Krieg*, p. 24.

[119] Particularly Ehud. The old narrative is "free of religious motivation" (Täubler, *Biblische Studien*, p. 22). "That Ehud as prophet was mistaken in regard to Eglon is sheer artifice" (R. Smend, *Lehrbuch der alttestamentlichen Religionsgeschichte* [2nd ed., 1899], p. 90, n. 1); if his journey to the quarries near Gilgal (Judges 3:19) has a special meaning, it is that he wants "to stimulate an oracle for Eglon" (R. Kittel, *Geschichte des Volkes Israel*, II, 117). Only H. Ewald calls Ehud a prophet (*Geschichte des Volkes Israel*, II, 527) and sees in him an "example of most vigorous prophetic activity long before Samuel" (p. 597); he finds his action, to be sure, "not quite worthy of a prophet" (p. 507, n. 2).

[120] So with Max Weber.

[121] So perhaps Smend, *Lehrbuch der alttestamentlichen Religionsgeschichte*, p. 61, n. 1.

[122] Compare, first of all, Judges 3:10; more difficult to judge are the places in the stories of Samson (Judges 13:25; 14:6, 19; 15:14).

[123] Compare W. Eichrodt, *Theology of the Old Testament*, I (1961), 308, n. 1. That "the few assured testimonies against the originality of this view" could "make one suspicious" (*ibid.*) is not very clear. Where else is it thought

still be without doubt a "correct interpretation."[124] Background[125] and broader effects[126] of the idea of cannot be pursued here where only the comparison with the minor judges is important. In connection with their administartion no mention is made of spiritual gifts. One has indeed become accustomed to speak of "charismatic jurisdiction,"[127] and naturally such a thing could have existed. However, we have no reason to assume it for the minor judges.[128] Even where one of these is known to us as charismatic (Deborah? Samuel? Jephthah), a necessary and generalizing connection does not become evident. The spirit of Yahweh overpowers the martial charismatic immediately before his deed, and after that certainly does not remain steadily at his disposal; it even leaves Saul, who was summoned to continuous conduct

---

to have been spoken of? Ewald misses the expression in the case of Ehud (*Geschichte des Volkes Israel*, II, 507, n. 2), but that is hardly the place for it; Buber in the case of Deborah (see above, pp. 59-60), but there are special circumstances at hand (compare Eichrodt, *Theology of the Old Testament*, I, 308-9).

[124] Smend, *Lehrbuch der alttestamentlichen Religionsgeschichte*, p. 61, n. 1.

[125] Buber, *Königtum*, pp. 139 ff., postulates in the period prior to the formation of the state a *Nabitum*, an association directed against the amphictyony of Joshua for the "reactualization of an alliance around a sanctuary into a politically active Israel" (p. 139). From this association the major judges had also come forth, for "the tradition of the pre-Davidic time knows . . . no other reception of the charisma than the prophetic; even the judge . . . must first of all become a prophet" (p. 142). I dare not agree completely with the extremely impressive thesis which reaches the goal desired by me much more fully and obviously than lies in my power in the present investigation; the exegetical basis seems to me too meager for the time being. If as much can be read between the lines of the Song of Deborah as Buber does, can one expect Amos (2:11) to have trustworthy knowledge of the past prior to the formation of the state; can one attribute to the story of Saul among the prophets beyond the anecdotal element, an "authenticity relating to the history of civilization" (Buber, p. 142)? For the time being there can be ascertained "for the old ecstatic movement . . . no correlation at all with the holy wars" (v. Rad, *Der Heilige Krieg*, p. 54).

[126] The spirit of Yahweh occurs later in kings, on the one hand, and in prophets, on the other.

[127] Compare Noth, *Laws*, p. 243 and the literature which is mentioned there on p. 244, n. 39.

[128] One cannot refer to a passage like Isaiah 11:2 ff. (compare 42:1), because, though it certainly connects the spirit of Yahweh and judging, it refers to an entirely different figure than that of the old judges.

of war (I Samuel 16:14). So much the less would those officials have possessed it by authority of their offices.[129]

---

[129] The ויקם "and there arose" in the case of Tola and Jair (Judges 10:1, 3), according to Hertzberg, *Beiträge zur Traditionsgeschichte und Theologie des Alten Testaments*, p. 123, signified something almost like a call by Yahweh. But the Qal does not have this meaning at all, and the evidence called upon by Hertzberg for proof in the Hiphil concerning Othniel, whom "Yahweh let arise" (Judges 3:9), moves the evidence concerning Tola and Jair rather into an unfavorable light. For Othniel was certainly no minor judge; the passage concerning him is Deuteronomic, and probably also 10:1aα (ולהושיע!). The ויקם in 10:3 may be an imitation of the former. That "naturally the view is not that these men had provided for the uprising on their own authority" is presumably correct, but as an argument here it is of little effect.

4

Ark and Central Sanctuary

The center of the amphictyony outside Israel is the central sanctuary. It is natural on the basis of analogy to assume the same for Israel. Unfortunately, clear statements in the Old Testament are not available.[1] Thus one is compelled to form a picture with the aid of inference from the state of affairs in a later time, guided by the analogy from the few reports which could afford some clues. In this way, Noth arrived at the thesis that the central sanctuary of the Israelite twelve-tribe confederation had been the Ark of Yahweh.[2] This thesis has found wide approval. If it is correct, then it means an argument against the separation of Yahweh war and the tribal confederation. For the Ark has played a part in the war of Yahweh.

This seems most obvious in Joshua 6 and I Samuel 4-6, thus in the case of the conquest of Jericho and during and after the lost battle with the Philistines. In Joshua 6, originally an etiological legend, the Ark to be sure appears only in appendixes which the legend in Joshua 3-4, on its own part also etiological, has attracted to itself.[3] The ground is firmer in I Samuel 4-6. The Ark certainly cannot be lifted out of this context; indeed it is its proper center and concern. But strictly speaking, the text is also not a historical source; "there are more stories than history; it is a popular

---

[1] Compare the statements of W. H. Irwin, *RB*, 72 (1965), 161 ff., which are in accord with the following in several instances.

[2] First set forth in *System*, pp. 95-96, 116 ff.

[3] Compare Noth, *Das Buch Josua*, pp. 31-32, 41; *Laws*, p. 142, n. 18; J. Maier, *Das altisraelitische Ladeheiligtum* (*BZAW*, 93 [1965], 21 ff.) .

rendering of history embellished by legend." [4] And the concentration upon the fate of the Ark has involved so much "that almost all of the accompanying circumstances, historically so important for us, have faded";[5] to the same extent it lessens the assurance that we can take the statements in this passage about the Ark itself at face value. What we have here is indeed the ἱερὸς λόγος of the Ark as it was told in Jerusalem at a time which was far removed, perhaps not in the number of years but certainly through historical upheavals of great proportion, from the events which constitute the background of I Samuel 4-6. Without question, one is correct if one calls the point "at which David can then intervene and again assign the Ark its proper place" (II Samuel 6), "historically certainly pertinent." [6] But the further one goes back from there, the less one can reckon with history. Little can be gained from I Samuel 4:3 ff. as an absolute invulnerable argument for the character of the Ark as a palladium of war. No more so, however, is the fact that the Ark was brought along only in the second battle and not earlier in the first (4:1-2) and that the Philistines said never before has the like happened (verse 7) a sufficient basis for the "impression that the Ark at that time was not being used as a true war standard" [7]—an impression which can be gained just from the sequence of Joshua 3-4 and 6. It would probably be too much to expect that the Ark was a "true war standard" in the sense that on the one hand its sole purpose of use was warlike and on the other that it was the standard in every war. A rigid dogma of this kind would have failed due to the reality. How should it be immediately available

---

[4] M. Dibelius, *Die Lade Jahwes* (*FRLANT*, 7 [1906], 113; compare furthermore L. Rost, *Die Überlieferung von der Thronnachfolge Davids* (*BWANT*, Vol. III, no. 6 [1926], pp. 41-42 ("Legende") ; v. Rad, Theology, I, 45 (closely connected with later fiction, "already some artistic construction") .

[5] v. Rad, *Der Heilige Krieg*, p. 28.

[6] So Hertzberg, *Die Samuelbücher* (1956) , p. 45.

[7] Dibelius, *Die Lade Jahwes*, p. 15; compare also H. Gressmann, *Moses und siene Zeit* (*FRLANT* NF, 1 [1913]) , 353; R. Hartmann, *ZAW*, 37 (1917/ 18) , 228.

in every war? [8] And if it embodied the presence of Yahweh in war, then it also did so in peace and had hardly less dignity here. However, if the war was the sphere in which the efficacy of the god was most perceptible and most characteristic,[9] then one certainly has the right to speak of the Ark according to its most important function, a palladium in war. That the two connected texts cited are indeed not adequate evidence in behalf of this function should be clear after what has been said up till now; especially not Joshua 6, or at least only in the sense that in later times such customs of use and operation were attributed to the Ark, to be sure not in accurate recollection of the conquering of Jericho, but perhaps of other events. This last applies to I Samuel 4-6, naturally *mutatis mutandis;* moreover, a particular event stands in the background here, even if only by chance more perceptible as to the *that* than as to the *how.*

Because of greater age, the so-called proverbs of the Ark in Numbers 10:35-36 have more value as sources. Their interpretation is controversial. The doubts as to whether the proverbs originally belonged together with the Ark[10] at all are perhaps exaggerated, but cannot be quite conclusively dispelled. The proverbs would always have been transmitted with some sort of contextual words, at least since the loss of their original *Sitz im Leben.* If so, then the name of Moses and the wandering situation are moreover a later insertion, rather than the Ark. Later, everything possible was brought into connection with Moses; a secondary reference to the Ark would indeed be more unusual. Raised beyond all doubt is that its sitation is that of Yahweh war: "Rise up, Yahweh,

---

[8] One therefore does not need to postulate its participation where it is not mentioned, hence in the battle Deborah; opposed to this, O. Eissfeldt, *ZAW,* Vol. 58 (1940/41), 191, n. 2, 199; Buber, *Königtum,* p. 134. Regular participation of the Ark in the war of Yahweh is indeed not to be expected at all by virtue of its particular character (see above, Chap. I). As for the ambiguity, compare also v. Rad, *Der Heilige Krieg,* p. 28, n. 45.

[9] See above, pp. 43-44.

[10] L. Rost, *ThLZ,* Vol. 85 (1960), column 724. Above all, Maier, *Das altisraelitische Ladeheiligtum,* pp. 8 ff.

that your enemies may be scattered and that the ones who
hate you may flee from before your countenance—Turn
back,[11] Yahweh, to (?) the multitudes[12] of Israel's thousands."
The situation of the wandering is not in principle ruled out
by that of the war, if one is thinking of a wandering in enemy
country. Apart from the setting the text to be sure does not
suggest that, and through the mention of Israel at the end
it becomes entirely questionable. For this name seems to
designate the association of the tribes only after the conquest
of the land. The proverbs would then belong to the time of
the Judges and would have been proclaimed aloud before
and after the battle at that time and possibly in the time of
the earliest kings.[13] The relatively late position of Numbers
10:29-36 [14] in the development of the tradition makes it appear quite possible that they have played their original role
a considerably long while before they were projected into
antiquity within the Pentateuchal narrative.

Similarly valuable in our connection would be the prov-
erb of the endless war between Yahweh and Amalek in
Exodus 17:16 if the כסיה of the Masoretic text should be the
correct reading and could be understood as כסא יה and if this
could be interpreted as a designation of the Ark with reference to Jeremiah 3:16-17.[15] This is quite conditional. From
Jeremiah 3:16-17 it certainly follows that the Ark has been

---

[11] Not much is gained by the usual conjecture שבה instead of שובה, nor
in connection with the idea of the throne. That at the outbreak of hos-
tilities Yahweh arises from the throne and at their cessation again sits upon
it (v. Rad, *Theology*, I, 307; *The Problem of the Hexateuch and Other
Essays* [1966], p. 110) is only one of the ideas which could be expected, and
not the most likely one. Compare K. Budde, *ZAW*, 21 (1909), 195; *ThSTKr*,
79 (1906), 495; Buber, *Moses* (2nd ed., 1952), p. 187 and n. 4—שוב is familiar for return from the war.

[12] Or "camps" (רבעות or ברבעות)? So Gunkel with Dibelius, *Die Lade
Jahwes*, p. 10.

[13] The word Israel could even argue for a beginning only in this time in
which the war of Yahweh was being fought by all Israel.

[14] Noth, *Überlieferungsgeschichte*, pp. 223-24.

[15] Compare O. Eissfeldt, *The Old Testament* (1965), p. 67, n. 9.

called the throne of Yahweh (כסא יהוה) ;[16] however, the passage is recent, post-Jeremianic,[17] and from it the bridge to olden times can be spanned only with difficulty. Rather than the explicit *designation* "throne of Yahweh," perhaps the *idea* of it; but even its age is uncertain and possibly does not reach back prior to Solomon.[18] If one wishes to hold fast to the Masoretic text in Exodus 17:16 and along with the tradition to find in it a throne, then an explanation of the throne in terms of the Ark is not without difficulties, although in any case it is more plausible than the explanation of the stony seat of Moses in verse 12; for it is a question of a battle cry which was certainly not uttered only once and at the same place;[19] the concept of a transportable object suggests itself.[20] That also holds true if נס is to be read instead of כס; the "standard of Yah" in verse 16 then could not be equated with the altar, "Yahweh is my standard," in verse 15; the assertions of the two verses in this instance also maintain a certain independence toward each other. According to this the difference between the readings כס and נס in verse 16 would not be too great. That the same word must stand [21] in both verses does not seem compelling to me; [22] the present adaptation is sufficient for a word play in Hebrew style—otherwise the Hebrew text could have established the equation which one presently conjectures. The derivation of נס from כס would

[16] The *tertium comparationis* between the Ark (verse 16) and Jerusalem (verse 17) could also be expressed more generally but the above understanding is the most likely. Negatively, Maier, *Das altisraelitische Ladeheiligtum*, pp. 67-68.

[17] Compare Rudolph on this passage.

[18] It appears at first to adhere to the cherubim rather than to the Ark. Regarding the problem, compare most recently E. Kutsch, *RGG*³ IV (1960), column 198.

[19] At this point Noth thinks of course of a certain "assembly place in the Amalekite battles," which, however, does not have to prove correct in light of the nature of the Amalekites as "non-settled elements" (Noth, *RGG*³ I [1957], column 302).

[20] If not wholly a purely figurative meaning of the word.

[21] Most recently Noth in *RGG*³, I, column 302.

[22] If so, then the changing of the word in verse 16 is the only possibility. "Yahweh is my throne" (as Beer *RE*, Vol. II, no. 1) would be incomprehensible.

be much more understandable than that of כס from נס. According to the sense, the statement "The hand upon the throne of Yahweh" would not be impossible if one thinks of the Ark.[23]

The argument of the divine name Yahweh Sebaoth is stronger if this is related to the Ark on the one hand and to the martial character on the other. Both are probable. The absence of the expression in Genesis-Judges[24] and its appearance here where it is a question of the Ark, or rather its location and the change of that location (I Samuel 1:3, 11; 4:4; II Samuel 6:2, 18; 7:8, 26-27), cannot be an accident. An often underrated difficulty, to be sure, lies in the fact that the predicate ישב הכרב׳ם is added to I Samuel 4:4 and to II Samuel 6:2, which can hardly be understood other than as a projection back of the conditions of the Solomonic temple.[25] What is true for the occupant of the cherubim throne could also be true for Yahweh Sebaoth. However, the difference between the Ark and the cherubim throne even at a later time is still so clear[26] that one is justified in taking Yahweh Sebaoth separately as the predicate of the older symbol and then also the name itself as older and therefore in any case as belonging to the Shiloh period.[27] As far as his warlike

[23] Against that II Samuel 6:6-7 would still be an objection, though certainly not a compelling one, considering that it is a question there of the etiological explanation of a place name and that both passages lie far apart from each other.

[24] Despite G. Beer, *RE*, Vol. II, no. 1, p. 1 (1920), column 1534, who following others, attributes this absence to a "purist editing." Now compare to that F. Baumgärtel in *Verbannung und Heimkehr* (Festschrift W. Rudolph [1961]), pp. 25-26.

[25] Compare H. Schmidt, *Eucharisterion* (*FRLANT* NF, Vol. I [1923]) no. 19, p. 143 among others. There are (except for the two passages mentioned) no indications justifying the assumption that there also existed in Shiloh a cherubim throne and that this one had been the model for that in the temple of Solomon (O. Eissfeldt, *Miscellanea Academica Berolinensia*, Vol. II, no. 2 [1950], pp. 144-ff.; M. Haran, *IEJ*, 9 [1959], 33).

[26] Compare on this point, above all, Haran, *IEJ*, 9: 32 ff.

[27] Eissfeldt takes both predicates together, at least one of which was originally Canaanite, and regards them as having been transferred together in Shiloh to the old Israelite Ark (*Miscellanea Academica Berolinensia*, II, 146 ff.). However, the union of the symbols is certain only for the time of

nature is concerned, we must here waive what some like
to cite as the chief reason for it,[28] namely the connection
with the Ark in its assumed warlike capacity; for we are
directly concerned about the accuracy of that presupposition.
Thus it depends upon the word itself.[29] As such in any case
it leaves open the questionable possibility, not only of
whether the צבאות is an earthly entity as one tends to assume,
but also of whether it is a heavenly one. The intervention of
celestial powers is directly decisive for the war of Yahweh in
Judges 5:20.[30] The שר־צבא־יהוה of Johusa 5:13 ff. with its
drawn sword creates a thoroughly martial impression, and
were it not here, as also at other times in the case of the
celestial host, for the sore point of the singular צבא instead of
the plural צבאות, then the obviously ancient passage could
already be regarded[31] as decisive. But after all, the plural
still seems rather to refer to the earthly multitudes of Israel,
even if the most conclusive evidence for that[32] is recent. Here

---

Solomon (according to Eissfeldt, p. 148, "Solomon" had them "repeated
with certain modifications in the temple at Jerusalem"), and the odd and
not particularly early passage in II Samuel 6:2 is, after all, perhaps not a
sufficient basis for such a far-reaching thesis (compare that also with pp. 129-
30 below). Arguing for a union of the title with the old Israelite Ark for the
first time in Canaan, V. Maag, *Schweizerische Theologische Umschau*, 20
(1950), 80, n. 1, states that it cannot be found in Genesis-Judges and also
not in the traditions "which concern themselves with the origin of the Ark."
But what kind of traditions are they?

[28] Compare W. Eichrodt, *Theology of the Old Testament*, I (1961), 192.

[29] To contest the martial character of the expression with the idea that
it is absent during the time of the Judges and preferred "in the time during
which Israel was not engaged in wars" (so L. Köhler, *Old Testament
Theology* (1957), p. 50, will not do. In the Book of Judges the Ark to which
it belongs does not appear either (see above p. 78 with n. 8), and later
application can be far removed from the original "Sitz im Leben."

[30] That the passage as "poetic hyperbole" has no power of proof is not
evident (E. Kautzsch, *PRE*[3] 21 [1908], 625). Compare also as ancient evidence
Joshua 10:12-13.

[31] With H. W. Hertzberg, *Die Samuelbücher* (1956), p. 33. According to
Maier, a "possibly later formation" is put forward in Joshua 5:14-15 (*Das
altisraelitische Ladeheitigtum*, p. 50, n. 75); Yahweh Sebaoth chiefly signifies
Yahweh as the God of the two levies of Israel and Judah, united under
David (p. 51). The absence of reliable pre-Davidic evidence and the usage
of צבאות in I Kings 2:5 seem to me not to substantiate this sufficiently.

[32] Above all, I Samuel 17:45. The parallel of the expression there has,
according to Buber, *Königtum*, p. 67, "a most authentic sound."

it does not depend at all upon a decision in favor of one of the two alternatives[33] or a development from one alternative to the other[34] or ultimately a combination of the terrestial with the celestial element;[35] our material does not seem to permit such a decision. The word may not always have had a rational explanation, naturally to be assumed at the beginning, however much some may then have wished to explain it rationally once more from time to time.[36] Such later explanations then attest nothing conclusive about the ancient meaning of the word. Concerning these, Psalm 24:8, 10, presumably the oldest evidence—besides the cited Ark-passages —also leaves us in the dark; concerning the sense of the title, however, it certainly reveals the most original evidence when it places יהוה צבאות in parallel with יהוה עזוז וגבור and יהוה גבור מלחמה.

Psalm 24 at the earliest belongs to the time of David, and it is this time also in which the connection of war and Ark, already sufficiently attested through the majority of the evidence cited in favor of a time prior to the formation of the state, steps into the bright light of history—and then quickly steps out of it again. Unfortunately the tradition does not portray the state of affairs for its own sake and therefore not in the fullness of detail and completeness in which one would like to see it described. In II Samuel 11:11 it is stated only incidentally (and for that reason it is even less suspect) that in the war against the Ammonites the Ark is in the camp with the levies of Israel and Judah.[37] That its being carried

[33] A third possibility would be Eissfeldt's proposal to understand צבאות as intensive plural abstract (*Miscellanea Academica Berolinensia*, II, 135 ff.). On the other hand, compare C. Brockelmann, *Hebräische Syntax* (1956), p. 16, n. 1; W. Eichrodt, *Theology of the Old Testament*, I, 193, n. 2; H.-J. Kraus, *Psalmen*, I (1960), 201.

[34] Thus, for example, B. H. Fredriksson, *Jahwe als Krieger* (1945), pp. 50 ff.; B. N. Wambacq, *L'épithète divine Jahvé Sebaôt* (1947).

[35] Thus perhaps Eichrodt, *Theology of the Old Testament*, I, 193; Buber, *Königtum*, p. 66 and n. 12.

[36] v. Rad, *Theology* I, 19.

[37] Moreover, possibly in II Samuel 10:12 ארן can be read for ערי (so A. Klostermann on this passage; O. Eissfeldt, *The Old Testament* [1965], p. 67).

along was in accord with the custom follows from II Samuel
15:24 where Zadok and Abiathar[38] "set it down" [38] during
the departure from Jerusalem obviously in order to follow
the march with it. According to verse 25, however, David
has it carried back into the city, in accord with the most
recent exegesis,[39] on the one hand because—as it indeed appears in the text—he leaves "the decision to the grace of God
in a way in which the oriental would perceive and express
it even today," and on the other because he sees "here a
possibility of being informed about the events in the city."
Both are believable, but both are also somewhat pale as an
explanation for the fact that David here, in contrast to other
times, waives the taking along of the security of the divine
presence into war. The decision must have been a more compelling necessity for David. Obviously the Ark was not suited
for what was at hand; taking it along would have been a
misuse of it. In II Samuel 11:11 it was stated: "The Ark and
Israel and Judah dwell in booths, but my master Joab and
the slaves of my master are encamped in the open field."
The Ark thus belongs together with the levies[40]; the mercenaries are encamped apart. What David has on his side in II
Samuel 15 are precisely the mercenaries and probably little
else (verses 14 ff.) ; the levies of Israel [41] stand on the other
side. The idea of employing the Ark of Yahweh against them
as against the Ammonites is impossible. Ammon can belong
to "Yahweh's enemies," but not Israel. Thus against Ammon
there can even be a war of Yahweh, but not against Israel.
In the "inner political altercation" between David and
Absalom the Ark has no place; [42] it belongs to the war of
Yahweh.

David claimed that he himself conducted "the wars of
Yahweh." Not only in the sense that he differentiated the

[38] Thus according to the improved text.
[39] Hertzberg, *Die Samuelbücher.*
[40] Compare moreover Alt, *Kleine Schriften* III, 240-41.
[41] According to Alt, *Essays*, p. 229, it concerns only the northern kingdom.
[42] v. Rad, *Problem*, p. 183. Similarly earlier Caspari, *ZWTh*, 54 (1912), 144.

private military expedition, the police raid as a דרך חל (I
Samuel 21:6), from the "holy war" [43] (compare also II
Samuel 11:11, 13), but he does so quite explicitly. In the
tradition of David's rise to power, Saul describes the fact
that David commands the Israelite levies (I Samuel 18:16) [44]
by saying that he "fights the wars of Yahweh" (verse 17) .[45]
The statement in the mouth of Abigail has less basis (I
Samuel 25:28) ; here David is still merely the leader of his
own mercenaries in ways which as far as Israel was concerned
must have appeared questionable. As a fully reliable statement about the present situation, the word of Abigail thus
does not come into consideration; but perhaps this can be a
postulate upon which claims and expectations for the future
are based, as Abigail says explicitly: "Yahweh shall certainly
prepare my lord a secure house, for my lord conducts the
wars of Yahweh." Whether or not the formulation is conceivable at this point of time and especially in the mouth of
Abigail,[46] its content has perhaps not been invented only
subsequently for the legitimization of David's claim of sover-
eign authority over all Israel. On the contrary, there are bases
for the fact that David—as irrational as it may sound to begin
with—even in the stage in which he was only the leader of his
mercenaries, could have claimed to a certain extent to conduct the "wars of Yahweh." Of course, not against Saul and
his people; he evades the fight against them altogether, and
the opportunity "to put forth the hand against the anointed
of Yahweh" he leaves constantly and emphatically unused
(I Samuel 24:7, 11; 26:9, 11, 23; compare II Samuel 1:14, 16).
But where it concerns the sworn enemy of Yahweh (Exodus
17:16, compare also Deuteronomy 25:17 ff.) , the Amalekites,

[43] Compare on this point Caspari, *Die Gottesgemeinde vom Sinaj und das
nachmalige Volk Israel* (*BFchrTh* 27, [1923], 21 and above all the more ex-
tensive conjectures of H. J. Stoebe, *Festschrift Friedrich Baumgärtel* (1959),
pp. 175 ff.
[44] Compare, in addition, Alt, *Essays*, p. 210.
[45] Compare, furthermore, I Samuel 17:47.
[46] On the other hand, compare Budde at this point.

there David executes the ban indeed not completely—that is to say, only against the people but not upon the remaining booty;[47] however, of this booty he sends portions to the elders of the cities of Judah with the express comment that it is "a present from the booty of the enemies of Yahweh" (I Samuel 30:26). The motivation for this act, in which political calculation without any doubt has at least a partial voice, he thus takes from the ideology of the Yahweh war: thus he obviously wants to say the possession of the booty of the enemies of Yahweh does not belong solely to its present conqueror but to those who are referred to at the end of the Song of Deborah (Judges 5:31) as אהביו in contrast to the איבי יהוה. Acting for them, he, David, has conquered the Amalekites; insofar as they can be reached they should all participate in the booty. This conduct of David during the lifetime of Saul, appointed by Yahweh to be the leader of the levies of all Israel, is very extraordinary. Perhaps in continuation of the old, in fact, particular, character of the war of Yahweh, David moves himself forward with the aim of being the advocate of this tradition until at some future time he himself as king should lead the war of Yahweh (besides the Ammonite pericope compare II Samuel 5:17 ff.; 8 with the strongest formulation in 5:24). In this context one can also understand his behavior toward the priestly line of the sons of Eli. This priestly line incurred the loss not only of the Ark but also of the sanctuary in Shiloh.[48] However, it had kept its role in the war of Yahweh as we can see from I Samuel 14 where Ahijah, the son of Ahitub, the son of Phinehas, the son of Eli, the bearer of the Ephod (verse 3),

[47] I Samuel 30:17 according to Wellhausen's conjecture להחרמם "instead of the linguistically doubtful and here either paradoxical or meaningless למחרתם" (J. Wellhausen, Der Text der Bücher Samuelis [1871], p. 144). Incompleteness of the ban also in Joshua 8:2, 27.

[48] The arguments against the identity of the priestly clan of Shiloh with the one of Nob (compare esp. E. Sellin, Geschichte des israelitisch-jüdischen Volkes, I [2nd ed., 1935], 144) does not seem to me to be effective if one takes into consideration the different character of the two traditions and sees the differences at least in part grounded therein.

is present at Saul's battle with the Philistines and is apparently supposed to obtain an oracle, but then does not (verses 18-19).[49] David seems to have gone to see the sons of Eli in Nob quite frequently for the purpose of oracles (I Samuel 22:15). During the emergency the visit in which the priest Ahimelech even renders material assistance to David and which reveals a close relationship going far beyond the usual extent (I Samuel 21:2 ff.) becomes fatal for the family: Saul hears about it and destroys the priests and the entire city of Nob (22:6-19). By taking the only survivor, Abiathar, into his house (22:20-23), David binds to himself the tradition of the family which was as venerable as it was important. Abiathar then performs for him functions analogous to those performed by Ahijah for Saul (23:9 ff.; 30:7-8; Abiathar inquires of God without being mentioned by name: 23:2, 4; II Samuel 2:1; 5:19, 23-24).

The solemn bringing of the Ark into Jerusalem (II Samuel 6) is the more important counterpart to the reception of Abiathar, and this fits logically into David's action.[50] Everything said underlines what Eduard Meyer remarked concerning the incident:[51] "With that, Yahweh of Hosts, the God of war, himself had taken his seat in the imperial city and set out from here in the wars of the people." No doubt one must agree with him when he continues: "And at the same time it was by means of Jerusalem's being thus represented as the successor of Shiloh that a broader connection with the traditions of Israel was effected."[52] The only thing problematical is whether we may further define this last point to say that (1) these traditions connected with the

---

[49] Text and exact meaning are unfortunately doubtful. One wonders if perhaps after all the Masoretic text, with its mentioning of the Ark despite 7:1 as over against the LXX, is somehow correct.

[50] Conjectures as to why David did not bring the Ark earlier and in which manner he arrived at it are superfluous.

[51] *Geschichte des Altertums*, Vol. II, no. 2 (3rd ed., 1953), p. 250. *Contra,* Maier, *Das altisraelitische Ladeheiligtum*, p. 63.

[52] Compare also O. Eissfeldt, *VT*, Supplement IV (1957), p. 142 and in other places.

Ark belonged to the sacred twelve-tribe confederation as such, and that (2) their adoption was connected with the Ark's being, from time immemorial, the central sanctuary of the confederation.

Arguing for the first, as Noth has demonstrated,[53] is the fact that in II Samuel 7, a tradition which in its beginning concerns the Ark-sanctuary and probably also as a whole has its place in it, the history of David is seen in continuity with that of the old tribal confederation, indeed just as David himself is "awarded a function in Israel, so also is the old sacred tribal confederation." [54] Apparently David is, according to this text, king of God's people Israel because he is master of the Ark-sanctuary in Jerusalem. The possession of the Ark according to that signifies something like an amphictyonic acknowledgment of legitimacy.[55] The idea that the Ark is therefore also the old central sanctuary is tempting. It does not seem compelling to me. We have seen[56] that in the course of the time of Judges, Yahweh war and tribal confederation approximated each other until at its end they virtually coincided. It would be no surprise if gradually in the course of the process or suddenly through a single event (I Samuel 4?) the role of the Ark had undergone a similar expansion into the amphictyonic as had the charismatic leadership.[57] Thus as the palladium of Yahweh Sebaoth it had indeed already long ago possessed a meaning which transcended the locality. The postulation of the institutional-amphictyonic element even in this weakened form is certainly not necessary. David needed the continuity with the past, and he may have taken what was offered to him. The Ark

[53] *Laws,* pp. 250 ff.

[54] *Ibid.,* p. 254.

[55] Against the view that under David the Ark "symbolized the old tribal confederation" (E. L. Ehrlich, *Geschichte Israels* [1958], p. 39) there can be no objection.

[56] See Chap. 1, above.

[57] See Chap. 3, above. Compare to that O. Eissfeldt, *ZAW,* 58 (1940/41), 199.

was, nevertheless, in any case, of the highest value. Subtle distinctions between these and those traditions and institutions of bygone times were hardly common property, and David would have guarded against resurrecting them again.[58]

If one cannot exclude these possibilities—and that seems to me to be the case—then it is necessary to examine the question of the relation between the Ark and the central sanctuary independently of the act of David.[59]

K.-H. Bernhardt [60] assumes the identity of the central sanctuary of the amphictyony after the conquest of the land with the sanctuary of the wandering tribes which had previously participated in the Sinai confederation. The latter must have been mobile and thus, according to the picture which the Hexateuch now presents, was the Ark. But this identity is not provable; the mobility of the central sanctuary, and thus also the necessity of identification as the Ark, cannot be postulated from this.

Also it need not follow from the high station which it possessed as "Yahweh's seat." "A second object of the Yahweh cult, closely corresponding to the Ark, put up at another place would bring about the danger of the disintegration

---

[58] If the Ark was the central sanctuary, then its being brought to Jerusalem by David was "a bold and in its legitimacy thoroughly questionable royal interference," for "in the cultic matters of the Israelite tribes, as king over the states of Judah and Israel, he had no immediate functions" (Noth, *Laws*, p. 134). It is different when it was a question of the homeless cult object of the destroyed temple of Shiloh to which David had already made himself an advocate insofar as he received the remnant of its priesthood in the person of Abiathar. While he wears the "linen Ephod" with the transference of the Ark (II Samuel 6:14), he seems to align himself in the tradition of the priesthood of Shiloh or of Nob (compare I Samuel 2:18; 22:18; furthermore 2:28; 14:3, 18 LXX; 21:10; 23:9; 30:7).

[59] Thereby it is presupposed that from the extra-Israelite analogies a central sanctuary of the Israelite tribal confederation may also be inferred. As already indicated above, this hypothesis is not provable. Over against this is the fact that the activity of the minor Judges, insofar as we can localize it, never took place at one of the sites where for other reasons the central sanctuary has been presumed. In this circumstance, naturally, an argument can also be conversely found against the amphictyonic character of the minor judgeship.

[60] *Gott und Bild* (1956), pp. 135 ff.

of the tribal confederation" (Bernhardt). How does one know that? We would have to be better acquainted than is the case with the structure of the tribal confederation and the nature and significance of its presumed central sanctuary.

Central sanctuaries have been suspected in Shechem, Bethel, Gilgal, and Shiloh. Shechem has the greatest probability for it.[61] But was the ark here? It is affirmed in Joshua 8:33. In the related older texts of Joshua 24; Deuteronomy 11:29-30; 27, there is no mention made of it,[62] and the conclusion can hardly be avoided that in Joshua 8:30 ff. "the Ark has been included only because of its role in Joshua 3, 4, 6." [63] Thus from this, one cannot interpret it [64] into the texts already mentioned as well as additional texts and events. That the assignment of the Ark to Shechem "is not only not suggested by our tradition but is actually excluded," [65] seems to me again to be said too much in the reverse direction— unless one would have the confidence in our tradition, that in it the conditions of the early period after the conquest of the land were to some extent sufficiently fixed and that above all the itinerary of the original book of Joshua retained exactly the route of those Israelites who brought along with them the Ark from the desert. The silence of the older sources does not make it impossible for the Ark to have been in Shechem, but it is unlikely and in any case unusable as an argument for the identity of the central sanctuary and the Ark.

If one understands from the passages referred to—which

[61] The reasons are given by Noth, *System*, pp. 93 ff.; *History*, pp. 91-92; also Alt, *Kleine Schriften*, II, 324 ff.

[62] Ewald sees in the words "before God" in Joshua 24:1 an allusion to the presence of the Ark (*Geschichte des Volkes Israel*, II [3rd ed., 1865], 584, n. 1). The phrase can be documented at many places in entirely corresponding usage where there can be no thought of the Ark.

[63] Noth, *History*, p. 93, n. 1. The suggestion, then, that a cultic act outside Jerusalem conflicts with the Deuteronomic ideology (K.-H. Bernhardt, *Gott und Bild*, p. 137; J. A. Soggin, *ZAW*, 73 [1961], 84) is, on the other hand, to no avail, quite apart from the fact that the Deuteronomists in pre-Solomonic times respect the cult at many points and their criticism begins only with Solomon.

[64] With Bernhardt, *Gott und Bild*, pp. 123-24.

[65] O. Eissfeldt, *ZAW*, 58 (1940/41), 193, n. 3.

were secondarily inserted into the Deuteronomic historical work, and it seems rightly so to me—that the confederation of the tribes was founded in Shechem, and if one also sees reflected in them a "regularly undertaken celebration which still took place long afterwards in front of the sacred stone in the terebinth sanctuary of Shechem and to which obviously belonged a public confession of Yahweh, a renewal of the confederation and a proclamation of legal maxims," [66] then it makes the hypothesis of a removal of the central sanctuary from Shechem in the time prior to the formation of the state more difficult. For if anything, then, that celebration seems to have been fundamental for the existence and life of the tribal confederation. In case of a transfer of the central sanctuary, it would really have had to go along. The persistency which "cultic celebrations, not only in their execution but also in the local tie to a certain place which they have once had, tend to maintain with great tenacity," and here apparently have maintained,[67] does not really compensate for the fact that the amphictyony, upon abandoning the center at Shechem, would have forfeited one of its essential, if not the most essential, life functions. Nevertheless it remains possible, and even if one should perhaps depend less firmly than is often the case today upon a survival abroad of the old Shechemite model with its well-known continued tie to its original site, then the transfer, either once or repeated, of the center of the amphictyony[68] is not to be entirely excluded. We are concerned here with this possibility only insofar as the Ark plays a role therein.

[66] Noth, *History*, p. 92.

[67] *Ibid.*

[68] Or a decentralization in the sense that there has never existed one amphictyonic sanctuary, but more than one at the same time? The Greek parallels which H. Wildberger, *Jahwes Eigentumsvolk* (AThANT, 37 [1960], 67) brings forward for this possibility are indeed only a small support for this. For there it is a question of the sanctuaries of different deities worshiped within one and the same amphictyony. For example, the co-existence of יהוה צבאות and יהוה אלהי ישראל does not even approximately constitute a counterpart to this polytheism.

H.-J. Kraus has postulated Gilgal as simultaneously the site of the central sanctuary and the Ark.[69] According to his supposition the מול הגלגל in Deuteronomy 11:30, which transferred the rites of Ebal and Gerizim (verse 29) to Gilgal,[70] speaks in favor of a transfer of the Shechemite rites to that place. This is tempting; however, the manner of expression remains unusual and forced and the supposition therefore unprovable, especially in view of the recent date of the text. The twelve stones in Gilgal (Joshua 4:20) will have actually symbolized the twelve tribes. Possibly they are also a clue to the collective Israelite significance of the site in the period just prior to the formation of the state (compare I Samuel 11:15; II Samuel 19:41 ff.).[71] It certainly proves correct that the Ark belongs to the presuppositions of the etiological history of Joshua 3:4.[72] But in what sense? Surely not in the sense that the Ark would have been there for a long time, but rather that it (according to the opinion of the narrator) was taken along in the conquest of the land and was thus also present here. A long stay of the Ark in Gilgal in later times—that is to say, after the postulated abandonment of the central sanctuary in Shechem and shortly before the creation of the state—cannot be established with this text. Neither can it be established with Judges 2:1 where one has suspected the Ark behind the angel.[73]

Bethel stands in a peculiar and a closer relation to the Shechemite rites than Gilgal if, as Alt[74] has made plausible, the narrative in Genesis 35:1 ff. reflects or even confirms etiologically a regularly undertaken pilgrimage at whose begin-

[69] *VT*, I (1951), 181 ff.

[70] *Ibid.*, pp. 193-94. Reasons from the history of the tradition argue on a larger scale for connections between Shechem and Gilgal; compare *ibid.*, pp. 186 ff.

[71] To that end Alt, *Kleine Schriften*, I, 184. Constructions of an entirely different kind by K. Möhlenbrink, *ZAW*, 58 (1940/41), 57 ff.

[72] Noth, *Josua* (2nd ed., 1953), p. 33.

[73] Smend, *Die Erzählung des Hexateuch* (1912), p. 274; O. Eissfeldt, *ZAW*, 58: 191, n. 2, p. 194; K. Galling, *ZDPV*, 75 (1959), 13 and n. 35.

[74] *Kleine Schriften*, I, 79 ff.

ning in Shechem one can recognize actions from the ceremonial of Joshua 24 (Genesis 35:2, 4; Joshua 24:14, 23).
Is a transfer of the amphictyonic central sanctuary assumed
here? The older one estimates the age of the tradition,[75] the
more readily one may accept it.[76] However, this is questionable.[77] If one searches in Israelite history for the "unknown
historical reasons" out of which fixed cultic acts were transferred from Shechem to Bethel,[78] then one will find them
most naturally and therefore most clearly with Alt [79] in the
elevation of the sanctuary of Bethel to the national sanctuary
by King Jereboam (I Kings 12:29 ff.). That is in harmony
with the composition of Genesis 35:1 ff. by the Elohist who
resided in the northern kingdom.[80] A comparable significance of the sanctuary of Bethel in the time of Judges cannot
be determined unless one relies upon Judges 20:18, 23, 26-
28; 21:2. Bethel undoubtedly is only subsequently inserted
into the context of Judges 19-21, so that the verses referred
to, so far as it is a question there originally of Bethel and
not Mizpah, are secondary.[81] Within these secondary verses
now stands the passages 27b-28aα, which in relation to them
is in turn secondary:[82] "The ark of the covenant of God was
there in those days, and Phinehas, the son of Eleazar, the son
of Aaron stood before it in those days." On behalf of the
historicity of this late gloss, it may be asserted that in view
of the fact that Mizpah in history was the assembly place of

[75] With Noth, *Überlieferungsgeschichte*, pp. 87-88.
[76] With Noth, *History*, pp. 94-95.
[77] That from here "no doubt in general the wandering motif, which was
then plentifully utilized has found entrance into the patriarchal narratives,"
(Noth, *Überlieferungsgeschichte*, p. 87) seems to me unprovable and more
unnatural than the usual explanation of this motif (compare H. Gunkel on
Genesis 12:8 and other places).
[78] Noth, *Überlieferungsgeschichte*, p. 87.
[79] *Kleine Schriften*, I, 87.
[80] *Ibid.*
[81] Compare esp. Noth, *System*, pp. 166-67.
[82] If it originally belonged here, it would appear in verse 18; 28aβ
necessarily belongs immediately after 27a. That is also the case if Hertzberg is correct at this point, that the entry here of Phinehas and the Ark
should emphasize "that it now moves toward the decision."

the tribes, no reason for the introduction of Bethel is discernible except for its role as the site of the Ark—its only role in that connection.[83] However, the latter is doubtful, for even in the Bethel verses the statement concerning the Ark (27*b*, 28*a*α) is only secondary. Thus one must differentiate between the two elements. The Ark entered after the introduction of Bethel.[84] Budde certainly gives the correct explanation of the passage: "The sacrifices at Bethel seemed to be too doubtful to a follower of P; he quickly brought the Ark of the covenant, which according to P stood in Shiloh (Joshua 18:1, compare I Samuel 4), over to Bethel in order to justify them. The Chronicler in II Chronicles 1:3-6 proceeds quite similarly with I Kings 3:4. The legitimate priest was added after an approximate calculation of the time." According to Eissfeldt[85] "in this case it is out of the question" for the statement "to represent an invention because it would be difficult to explain how, contrary to the reality, the Ark was later brought into connection with Bethel, which as the site of the cult of a rival deity was greatly detested." But when the mantle falls, the Duke must follow: once Bethel was in the history, the temporary placing of the Ark there apparently seemed to the commentator to be the lesser evil as compared to an illegitimate cult of all Israel. That Bethel itself came in can in turn be best explained from its role as the national sanctuary since the time of Jeroboam.[86] An incidental reference to the former character of Bethel as the seat of the amphictyonic central sanctuary and of the Ark[87] stands or falls with the probability which one still wishes to attribute to this character after all that has been said.

[83] Noth, *History*, p. 94 and n. 3.

[84] The contrary, as H. Strauss, *Untersuchungen zu den Überlieferungen der vorexilischen Leviten* (Dissertation, Evangelical Theological Faculty, Bonn 1960), p. 177, n. 360, discusses it, is impossible.

[85] *ZAW*, 58 (1940/41), 198.

[86] Correctly so, Strauss, *Untersuchungen zu den Überlieferungen der vorexilischen Leviten*, p. 109; compare also K. Galling *ZDPV*, 67 (1943), 31.

[87] Strauss, *Untersuchungen zu den Überlieferungen der vorexilischen Leviten*, n. 360.

The foregoing also does not favor the ingenious and stimulating hypothesis of J. A. Soggin:[88] the Ark was taken along on the piligrimage from Shechem to Bethel whence the "terror of God," which according to Genesis 35:5 falls upon the surrounding cities, can be explained. One cannot really maintain that the terror of God "adheres only to the ark";[89] the expression חתת אלהים, indeed the noun חתה, after all, is encountered only in our passage, the related nouns חתחתים and חתית only in completely different contexts, the verb חתת nowhere where the Ark is mentioned. The thing these words describe, the confounding of the enemies by Yahweh so that they are powerless, occurs quite frequently without the Ark;[90] the passages where the Ark participates causatively[91] are not the most characteristic ones. Essentially the verse in my opinion refers to Chapter 34 rather than to the quite peaceful incident in 35:2-4; as that which connects the two passages[92] it is especially easily understood, even if the Septuagint version is correct with which Soggin[93] wishes to prove it to be the original conclusion of 35:2-4. Even so, the Ark cannot be claimed for Shechem and Bethel.

On the other hand it surely stood in Shiloh.[94] Was Shiloh also a central sanctuary? Albright[95] even considers it to be the only one. But at least the priority of Shechem should be adhered to.[96] The significance of Shiloh for all Israel is

[88] *ZAW*, 73 (1961), 78 ff. Compare even earlier C. A. Keller, *ZAW*, 67 (1955), 150.

[89] Soggin, *ZAW*, 73: 80.

[90] Compare v. Rad at this point and *Der Heilige Krieg*, p. 12.

[91] Soggin, *ZAW*, 73: 80.

[92] Thus v. Rad at this point.

[93] *ZAW*, 73: 79-80.

[94] For the fact that it was always there, most recently E. Nielsen, *Shechem* (2nd ed., 1959), p. 36, n. 1.

[95] W. F. Albright, *Archaeology and the Religion of Israel* (3rd ed., 1953) pp. 103 ff; compare also *From the Stone Age to Christianity* (2nd ed., 1957) pp. 281-82. Accordingly, for example, G. E. Wright, *Biblical Archaeology* (2nd ed., 1962), pp. 89-90. On the other hand, Irwin, *RB*, 72: 117.

[96] That Shiloh has replaced Shechem has been repeatedly advocated by E. Sellin (most recently: *Geschichte des israelitisch-jüdischen Volkes*, I [2nd ed., 1935], 138) with reference to a Samaritan tradition according to which Eli fled with the Ark from Shechem to Shiloh.

asserted in passages such as Joshua 18:1; 21:2; Judges 21:12, 19; I Samuel 1:3, 7; 2:22 [97]—not all of these are particularly old, so they are not reliable, especially when one inquires beyond the general impression as to whether Shiloh not only held significance for all Israel but also precisely amphictyonic status. On behalf of the latter I know of no evidence,[98] though it is certainly possible. In view of the politicizing of the amphictyony which takes place within the later period of the Judges on the one hand and in view of the expansion of the Yahweh war into the national war on the other, it is not even improbable, regardless of whether or not the Shechemite rites at the same time maintained their function in the old manner. The fact that the Ark was situated in Shiloh could by all means have been influential on behalf of the transfer.[99] Perhaps the probable state of affairs may be formulated with Friedrich Horst's criticism of Noth's "System der zwölf Stämme Israels" [100] in effect "that the Ark as a special sanctuary of the 'house of Joseph' belonged from the outset to the latest founding of the temple in Shiloh, that in time Shechem was pressed back to such an extent by Shiloh that the cult of Shiloh received the position of the amphictyonic cult and then the Ark passed over into the possession of the amphictyony."

[97] May one accept Genesis 49:10 as ancient evidence? Compare on this point most recently v. Rad, *Old Testament Theology,* II (1965) , 12-13.

[98] That Samuel's function as a judge took place at different places, Weiser, *Samuel (FRLANT,* 81 [1962], p. 11) traces back to the preceding destruction of the central sanctuary in Shiloh. We do not know, however, whether Samuel would otherwise have been active in Shiloh (his childhood story in I Samuel 1 ff. provides no useful evidence in that respect) and even that would still be no proof; for there, where we know the places of the Judges' activity, the central sanctuary was not involved (see above, pp. 58-59; 89, n. 59) .

[99] Proceeding from the supposition that the number twelve of the tribes has supported the tending of the central sanctuary in rotation, Noth asks if, in the case of the permanent priesthood in Shiloh, it was not a question "of a more recent innovation" (*Festschrift Bertholet* [1950], p. 414) . However, as an argument against the amphictyonic character of Shiloh, this is not sufficient.

[100] *Theologische Blätter,* Vol. 12 (1933) , columns 106-7.

Even that cannot be proved. Thus one has all the less reason to discern in the Ark the amphictyonic central sanctuary for the earlier period. The result of this chapter, therefore, does not refute the separation of the war of Yahweh and the tribal confederation.

5

Rachel Tribes and Leah Tribes

The Ark was in Shiloh in the region of Ephraim, or of Joseph. Therefore it is certainly correct to regard it as a sanctuary belonging at first especially to this tribal region.[1] That it had been Benjaminite, as has been presumed for various reasons,[2] has over against this less likelihood. It can scarcely be determined if the Ark already appeared in the tradition of the conquest of the land in Joshua 2 ff. when this was still particularly Benjaminite. If so, then naturally an indication would be provided of a relationship to the Ark claimed by Benjamin at least for the past. But then one may not take Joseph and Benjamin as alternatives; for in any case the Ark has to be accounted for in Shiloh and the alternative can

[1] Compare B. Stade, *Geschichte des Volkes Israel*, I (1887), 458; M. Debelius, *Die Lade Jahwes*, pp. 119-20; Noth, *System*, p. 96; O. Eissfeldt, *ZAW*, 58: 199. That the Ark had been "the" tribal sanctuary of Ephraim or even of Joseph is therewith not said. We do not know if such was the case at all, and in our situation the circumstance that after the loss of the Ark in the battle with the Philistines neither Ephraim nor Joseph makes any obvious attempt to recover it indicates the contrary. As for the significance for all Israel from the outset, this, however, says nothing (contrary to L. Couard, *ZAW*, 12 [1892], 79-80). Furthermore, the association of the Josephite Joshua with the Ark as it confronts us in Joshua 2 ff., in view of the complicated question of the originality of the figure of Joshua in that (chiefly Benjamite) connection, is no useful argument for the stated thesis, even though this was at first based upon it; compare Wellhausen, *Prolegomena*, p. 45.

[2] E. Sellin, *Alttestamentliche Studien R. Kittel zum 60. Geburtstag.* (*BWAT*, 13 [1913]), 184 ff. in any event for the Tabernacle on the basis of an uncertain interpretation of Deuteronomy 33:12; relating this interpretation exclusively to the Ark and questioning the identity of Shiloh and *chirbet selun* is R. Hartmann, *ZAW*, 37 (1917/18) 215, 237; taking esp. the role of the Ark in Joshua 2-9 and interpreting it in his own way is E. Nielsen, *VT*, Supplement VII (1960), pp. 61 ff.

even then only be called: Joseph or Joseph and Benjamin. Despite a certain predominance of the former of the two probabilities, no great disadvantage is created by the fact that a reliable decision cannot be made. Some kind of closer connection between Joseph and Benjamin within Israel as a whole is, in any case, already indicated in that Joseph and Benjamin are considered to be the sons of Rachel. From that one may believe them capable of a common existence in one way or the other and need not necessarily understand every possession of the one too exclusively in relation to the other. Now be that as it may in the case of the Ark, its connection to Joseph or the tribes of Rachel brings us to the question of whether this connection also corresponds to a special relationship of this group of tribes to the war of Yahweh. One may not dismiss this possibility as a matter of course, especially after what has been said above about the originally sectional character of the war of Yahweh, and one may regard the possession of the Ark at the same time as a prime positive indication.

As a relation of Manasseh, the charismatic leader Gideon is Josephite. It seems certain that in his battle he also summoned Ephraim while it cannot be held probable for the other tribes.[3] The Ephraimites appear here (Judges 8:1-3), moreover, in the role of the fiercest warriors who are insulted that they were not asked to participate right from the beginning.

They appear quite similarly also in connection with Jephthah's victory over the Ammonites (Judges 12:1-6). No matter how the two passages stand in relation to each other,[4] the duplication already indicates the fact that the Ephraimites thought of themselves as a permanent constituent in the quota of such wars; at least that is what was said of them. And when in view of the victory of Jephthah and his Gileadites the word proceeds from an Ephraimite mouth that the

---

[3] See above, pp. 19-20.
[4] See above, p. 21, n. 23.

Gileadites are "fugitives from Ephraim" and Gilead lies "in the midst of Ephraim and in the midst of Manasseh" (Judges 12:4), therein lies also the claim to competence in conducting the war of Yahweh. At the same time, Jephthah is nevertheless Ephraimite[5] in the broader sense, so that we may view his charismatic leadership as standing completely within the Josephite tradition.

Ephraimites seem to have come to the aid of the Benjaminite Ehud in the battle against the Moabites; at least it is most likely that the expression in Judges 3:27, "hill country of Ephraim," which could if necessary also mean solely Benjaminite territory, is to be understood in this sense.[6]

It appears similarly—and in so doing we move already beyond the actual time of Judges—in Saul's first battle against the Philistines according to I Samuel 14:23 in the LXX.[7]

In the latter two cases mentioned, Benjamin has the initiative. The narratives of the conquest of the land in Joshua 2 ff.[8] supply equally as strong a picture of the strength with which the concept of the war of Yahweh[9] still lived on in this tribe as of the charismatic leadership of Saul.

Here one may certainly refer also to the further history of the northern Israelite kingdom in which the charismatic leadership never quite ceased to exist.[10] The first king, Jeroboam, was Ephraimite (I Kings 11:26), and he was appointed by the prophet Ahijah of Shiloh (verse 29).

---

[5] Compare on that point also Noth, *ZDPV*, 75 (1959), 61, n. 113.

[6] Compare above, p. 20.

[7] See above, p. 24.

[8] In Joshua 10 it is then again a question of Ephraim; compare Alt, *Kleine Schriften*, I, 134, n. 3; pp. 187-88. Alt discusses the participation of Benjamin, *ibid*, p. 188.

[9] It is indeed not identical with the historicity of the narratives.

[10] Compare Alt, *Essays*, p. 243. In later times the Israelite kingdom in my opinion is not so much disposed to the pattern as is proposed by Alt. However, the principle and the origin of the phenomenon are little affected by it.

It could now appear as though the classical war of Yahweh in the classical period does not fit the pattern. In the battle of Deborah, as seems to follow from their sole mention in Judges 4:6, 10, and their double entry in the Song of Deborah (5:14, 15, text emended 18), Zebulun and Naphtali bear the main burden of the battle. The leading personalities come from Naphtali (4:6) and Issachar (5:15). On the other hand, the tribes of Rachel are not mentioned at all in the prose account and only once in the Song, in contrast to the tribes which were chiefly concerned and active. But so much for that! Except for the tribes for which there was no possible choice, namely Zebulun, Naphtali, and Issachar, the ones that participate are the tribes of Rachel and no one else. Moreover, and this is hardly less important, the initiative emanates from Deborah, who is indeed Issacharite but who resides in the hill country of Ephraim and lives in the midst of the tribes which usually lead the wars of Yahweh. If one may connect the all-Israelite program of the Song of Deborah with the collective Israelite office of the Judge,[11] then one can just as well associate her summons to war with her place of residence.[12] Thus viewed, the victory over the Canaanites appears to be the result, if one wishes, of a fortuitous state of affairs, but that still does not make the supposition improbable.

The example of the battle of Deborah proves that the prerogative of the Rachel tribes with regard to the war of Yahweh does not imply a restriction to these tribes. Such a restriction would indeed be preposterous, and if it did exist at one time, then it was abolished at the latest by Deborah. Naturally the objection that the tribes of middle Palestine are the ones of which we know the most and that, in the case of the other tribes, if we had more and better traditions of them, perhaps the war of Yahweh would appear just as clearly, should be taken seriously and not strictly rejected.

[11] See above, pp. 57-59.
[12] Compare Täubler, *Biblische Studien*, p. 139.

Nevertheless it has to be pointed out that the grudging treat-
ment of the other tribes in our sources can be explained, not
only in terms of geographical factors, but in that there was
just not as much to tell of them as there was of the Rachel
tribes. And what was told was quite overwhelmingly the warlike deeds.

Even though considering the prominent communication in the Song of Deborah, which is not in every instance
valid as an objection, the positive proof of the wars of Yahweh in the case of the other tribes would be more important.
This proof can be shown, in my opinion, only with great
difficulty. To actions such as those of the Calebite Othniel
(Judges 3:9-10) the historian can attribute no importance
whatever; evidently Othniel appears just so that the sequence
of savior figures in the Book of Judges might be opened
by a representative of the southern tribes.[18] Even if arche-
ology should make a military conquest of Hazor by Israelite
alliances likely, nothing positive would be ascertained about
its character as the war of Yahweh, not to mention the
historicity of the tradition of Joshua 11 in its present form.
The only quotation of the "Book of the Wars of Yahweh"
(Numbers 21:14) seems to concern an event which has
occurred not in the territory of the tribes of Rachel but in
that of Reuben or Gad; however, the tribes of Rachel also
had disputes with Moab in the period of the Judges; moreover, the sense of the quotation is "completely obscure," [14]
and we are not in a position to say how it got into the "Book
of the Wars of Yahweh" and in which connection it stood
there, just as indeed on the whole practically no useful clues
exist for the determination of the age and content of this
book.[15] The passage therefore is no counter-argument.

[18] Wellhausen, *Prolegomena*, p. 232. The sequence of anecdotes in Judges
1:1 ff. has scarcely greater value for our context.

[14] Noth, *ZAW*, 58 (1940/41), 175.

[15] Compare finally A. H. J. Gunneweg, *Mündliche und schriftliche Tradition der vorexilischen Prophetenbücher* (*FRLANT*, 73 [1959]), 29.

Weightier still is another doubt which von Rad [16] has about
the originally Josephite character of the war of Yahweh,
namely, that the battle of the Amalekites in Exodus 17:8 ff.
is to be fixed as to time evidently early and as to location in
the vicinity of Kadesh. Von Rad would like to see the Leah
group, which was already linked amphictyonically, or part of
it, fighting on the side of Israel. Even if with this, the supposition—which in my opinion is incorrect—of a necessary
amphictyonic background of a "holy war" plays a part, the
fact remains that the Amalekites are intelligible to us geo-
graphically only as neighbors of Judah and of the tribes connected with it in the south, but not of the tribes in middle
Palestine (compare Genesis 14:7; Numbers 13:29; I Samuel
27:8; 30:1). Certainly the Benjaminite Saul comes into conflict with them (I Samuel 15), but in his role as King of
Israel, and the scene seems to have been situated far to the
south.[17] On the other hand, the fact must be remembered
that the Amalekites were "unsettled peoples" [18] and that they
could very well have met elements of the tribes which later
settled in central Palestine during the wandering of the latter
in the desert. Thus, this text cannot with the necessary certainty be claimed as positive testimony for a Yahweh war
independent of the tribes of Rachel.[19]

   Ultimately opposed to all objections is what is said about
Joseph in the blessing of Jacob. According to Genesis 49:23

----

[16] *Der Heilige Krieg*, p. 17.

[17] The place טלאים (I Samuel 15:4), if it is identical with the site טלם
(Joshua 15:24), lay under Josiah in the southernmost district of the Kingdom of Judah.

[18] Noth, *RGG*[3], I (1957), column 302.

[19] Just as unlikely is the war of the Judean David against the Amalekites
(I Samuel 30). It falls in a time in which even the originally nonhomog-
eneous tribes have already diversely influenced each other, and in the case
of David as the follower of Saul, such influence will have been especially
strong. Perhaps beyond that, in the rigorous conception of the ban com-
mandment in I Samuel 15 by Samuel and in its much more lax handling
through David in I Samuel 30, one may see a proper and an improper way
to lead the war of Yahweh, wherein would appear the less important tradition which it had in the south. Also see above, pp. 85-86.

"archers" made war upon the tribe. By these are now pretty generally understood no longer the Aramaeans of Damascus[20] but the nomadic opponents of the time of the Judges.[21] Joseph has triumphed with divine help; at least that is the sense of the textually difficult verse 24. The conception of the war of Yahweh is as clear as day.[22] Even more important then is verse 26 where Joseph is called the נזיר אחיו.[23] The position of superiority which is thereby attributed to him does not, as again is today almost generally accepted, consist in the kingship.[24] According to the Samson narrative the נזיר was a man who "was a champion and partisan of Israel who upon his own responsibility led the wars of Yahweh." [25] Joseph was precisely this according to our passage in the sense of a distinction and of having been singled out from his brothers, and most certainly not only in a single instance,[26] but in general. Thus the affirmation expresses with all desirable clarity what had already manifested itself to us in the consideration of the narratives: Joseph's direct and the other tribes' more remote and rather derived relationship to the war of Yahweh. It is especially valuable that it also indirectly gives expression to this last point, for in the narratives it could be inferred only with the help of the *argumentum e*

[20] Thus, according to Wellhausen, many in his time, *Prolegomena*, p. 323.

[21] The reasons esp. in Gunkel *in loc*. That the raids of the Midianites, to which Gideon with 300 men put an end, are not sufficient for an explanation (Wellhausen, *Composition*, p. 324) is no doubt correct; but, after all, certainly a characteristic and hence also repeated situation is presupposed. A reference just to the battle of the Philistines in I Samuel 7 (so Täubler, *Biblische Studien*, pp. 209 ff.) seems to me by no means justified.

[22] Compare Gunkel and v. Rad *in loc*.

[23] Just as in Deuteronomy 33:16.

[24] So Wellhausen, *Composition*, p. 324, and many others.

[25] Gunkel *in loc*. Compare also the literature cited therein. According to Sellin-Rost, *Einleitung in das Alte Testament* (9th ed., 1959), p. 48, the expression labels the tribe "as that which is consecrated to the constant battle along with Yahweh."

[26] That the designation aims especially at the wars of Saul (K. Galling, *RGG³* III [1959], column 860) in my opinion also fails in that rather Benjamin played such a role there.

silentio and from the isolated situation of the battle of Deborah.

As we have already seen, Joseph was distinguished at this point less from Benjamin[27] than from the large majority of the tribes. Between the two tribes there existed a community and even a common interest in the leading of the wars of Yahweh, of course only from case to case and not on a permanent basis, but it was indeed a question of autonomous tribes.[28] It is even more remarkable that this relationship did exist, and it is also an indication of the fact that the genealogical combination of the two as sons of Rachel could have grounds in a common past above and beyond the geographical proximity in the arable land. Circumstances being what they are, such things are not provable; and it can well be that in the beginning the proximity of the two Canaanite "leagues of cities" [Städteriegeln] in the land west of the Jordan led to mutual contact, influence, and no doubt to a contractual union.[29] That the conquest of the land in the case of both tribes, however, obviously took place, as to time, following that of the tribes of Leah,[30] and as to locality from the same direction,[31] could reflect a community already during this process, without entailing the thesis of the secondary separation of Benjamin from Joseph.[32] The breaking-off of the sequence of Joshua legends at the border of the territory of Benjamin certainly suggests that in the case of these legends it was originally a question of the special tradition of Ben-

[27] The passage concerning Benjamin in the Blessing of Jacob (Genesis 49:27) to be sure certainly has highway robbery in mind and not the war of Yahweh; compare Gunkel at this point. *Contra,* see Täubler, *Biblische Studien,* pp. 215 ff.

[28] The subdividing of Joseph into Ephraim and Manasseh (or Machir) need not occupy us here. Both divisions were familiar with the war of Yahweh. Also compare on this problem Alt, *Kleine Schriften,* I, 163, n. 1.

[29] Compare Noth, *System,* p. 37, n. 2 (with antiquated evidence), p. 66; Alt, *Kleine Schriften,* I, 164-65, 188.

[30] Compare Alt, *Kleine Schriften,* I, 162 ff.

[31] Noth, *History,* p. 74; *Überlieferungsgeschichte,* pp. 56-57.

[32] Compare against this, Alt, *Kleine Schriften,* I, 164, n. 4.

jamin, perhaps of the sanctuary of Gilgal.[33] But that is evidence from the history of tradition from which one need not draw the historical conclusion that Joseph and Benjamin had not participated in a joint conquest of the land. The role which two obviously Ephraimite factors play in this Benjaminite sequence of legends, the person of Joshua[34] and the symbol of the Ark, advises against such a conclusion. If we could reach beyond the present form of the sequence and reconstruct its Benjaminite form, more could be said about it; even though in view of the fact that a community could have been assumed between Joseph and Benjamin which came into being only in the arable land, that still does not answer everything. For the period prior to the conquest of the land everything remains yet more unresolved. Since there seems to be no possibility other than pure speculation of deciding the question or even of approaching the decision as to whether and to what extent one can already speak here of the tribes of Rachel or even of Joseph and Benjamin, in the next chapter, which is concerned with this period, I use the expression "tribes of Rachel" where in reality it could also have been a matter of Joseph alone (or possibly Benjamin) —of course, also of elements which were merged in the later "house" of Joseph, but elements which became decisive for its life and thought.

The insolubility of this problem does not need be too troublesome to us, however, where it is a question of the common position of Joseph and Benjamin within the twelve-tribe confederation. One may characterize this on the basis of what has been said up to now, namely that the tribes of Rachel represented the element of the war of Yahweh in the amphictyony—by which naturally not everything is supposed to be said about them, but what is ascertained is also not trivia. The logic of our inquiry suggests it be continued here

[33] *Kleine Schriften,* I, 187.
[34] So Noth, *System,* pp. 82-83.

with the thesis: the element which the Leah tribes contributed was the "amphictyonic." I believe that this thesis not only fits into the context but also proves historically correct, and therein I rely upon Noth's thesis of the six-tribe amphictyony which the tribes of Reuben, Simeon, Levi, Judah, Zebulun, and Issachar formed in the period prior to the conquest of the land by Joseph and Benjamin.[35] The principle, system, and compass of the amphictyony were derived accordingly from the arable land [36] or already existed there in any case when the units which were not yet linked in this manner joined others already there, and from the addition resulted what constituted Israel in the following period. The activity in connection with the merger toward the larger twelve-tribe amphictyony, if one sees[37] in the "provincial Diet of Shechem" in Joshua 24 the act by which it was established, certainly appears not to have lain on the side of the Leah tribes; for here, if one can place confidence in the account which indeed passes silently over important aspects of the surmised event, the Josephite Joshua acts with complete supremacy.[38] And acting in the joint Israelite and thus understood amphictyonic sense is also subsequently, when we hear of it, a concern of the Rachel tribes rather than of the Leah tribes. However, that need not seem strange because, as was pointed out above in Chapter 2, the historical action is certainly not characteristic of the amphictyonic system as such. And even Joshua could not make the amphictyony into the vehicle of the historical act in the most

[35] Noth, *System*, pp. 75 ff.; *History*, pp. 89-90.

[36] That this must have been the case, one could also infer at the outset from the Greek analogy where it is indeed clearly a question of alliances in the arable land (compare E. Nielsen, *Shechem* [2nd ed., 1959], p. 35, n. 3). However, this argument is not sound, for in Israel's immediate proximity there exist groups of twelve and of six which were not firmly settled elements (Genesis 22:10-24; 25:13-16; 36:10-14; 25:2; 36:20-28 text emended; compare Noth, *System*, pp. 43-44).

[37] With Noth, *System*, pp. 65 ff.; v. Rad, *Theology*, I, 16-17; more cautiously, Noth, *History*, pp. 93-94.

[38] Compare at this point also Alt, *Kleine Schriften*, I, 191-92.

eminent sense, namely of the war of Yahweh; the tribes of Rachel acted "on their own responsibility" according to Yahweh's command and with his miraculous help, and only special circumstances helped them to convey their enthusiasm and energy to the group of dignitaries of the six tribes.[39]

[39] Noth suspects (*System*, p. 76) that these still possessed certain rights of reservation.

6

The Exodus from Egypt and the Formation of the Covenant at Sinai

Historical thinking tends to pursue phenomena into their past, even to their origin if possible, in order to understand them correctly. In the case of the war of Yahweh this is particularly difficult. It is present in the arable land. Does its origin also lie here? One might thereupon almost like to withdraw in resignation or in a *non liquet* when one remembers that according to Alt's statements,[1] which are not yet outdated, the conquest of the land by the Israelites proceeded, at least in its first stage, not militarily but peacefully, and that the most recent Pentateuchal criticism has made the historian's grasp of the period prior to the conquest of the land extremely difficult. If one considers the situation of the tribes between the conquest of the land and the creation of the state, it is also quite plausible that, as W. F. Albright[2] expresses it, "under such conditions Israel became martially minded and Israel's God became 'Yahweh, God of (the) Hosts (of Israel),' one of whose primary functions was to defend His people against foes whose only aim seemed to be to destroy it utterly and to devote it to their impure gods." And preference is certainly given to W. Caspari's[3] repeatedly proposed thesis of the essentially unwarlike life of the Bedouin before the conquest of the land, as over against the

---

[1] *Kleine Schriften*, I, 126 ff.

[2] *From the Stone Age to Christianity* (2nd ed., 1957) , p. 287.

[3] *ZWTh*, 54 (1912) , 110 ff.; *Die Gottesgemeinde vom Sinaj und das nachmalige Volk Israel* (1923) , pp. 15, 119-20.

proposition of H. Guthe[4] that the events in the wilderness took place "solely in war." But such general considerations do not exclude the fact that one may count upon the war of Yahweh in one form or another already prior to the conquest of the land, and indeed not only Albright but also Caspari does that. It is only that general arguments even in this direction, as one by all means can have them, cannot be decisive but can only hold the matter in abeyance. Is there a real clue?

Certainly there is, namely in the Song of Miriam in Exodus 15:21*b* (1*b*). In this case, and this enhances its value exceptionally in our context, it is a question of the only document in the Pentateuch, the character of which being to some extent contemporaneous with the events is indeed nowhere contested,[5] so that it possesses something like a direct source value. It is not as though it were a report of a witness who explains the event in such a way that it would be clear and capable of being reconstructed for us, but yet it is of such value that we possess a very early interpretation of what remains historically obscure[6] for us. And this interpretation explains the incident at the Reed Sea as a war of Yahweh. It is not true that one could just as well take it in a peaceable sense as in a military sense[7]; for even if Yahweh really intervened by means of a "strong north wind" (Caspari), nevertheless it is certainly a question of a deliverance from the peril of an enemy in which he "threw" the military power ("horse and charioteer") "into the sea." In principle this is in no way different from that in the Song of Deborah. There indeed the Israelite heroes only come "to the aid of

---

[4] *Geschichte des Volkes Israel* (1899) , p. 32.

[5] Compare R. Smend, *Das Mosebild von Heinrich Ewald bis Martin Noth* (1959) , p. 10.

[6] Otto Eissfeldt wonders whether the deliverance had at first been ascribed to Baal Zephon (*Baal Zephon, Zeus Kasios und der Durchzug der Israeliten durchs Meer* [1932], pp. 66 ff.) ; compare over against that, Hempel, *Gott und Mensch im Alten Testament* (2nd ed., 1936) , p. 33, n. 2 and other places.

[7] So Caspari, *ZWTh*, 54 (1912) , 128.

Yahweh" (Judges 5:23),[8] and it is he who is here as well as there glorified by the hymn. It will not do in the presence of this decisive factor to make anything of the difference of the means which Yahweh uses in the two instances for the purpose of destroying his enemies. This is confirmed by the more recent "Song of the Reed Sea" (Exodus 15:1-18), which calls the Yahweh of the Song of Miriam the "man of war" (verse 3) and looks upon his action in this place (verses 4-10) as having continued without interruption in the later wars of Yahweh (verses 14-17). It is understood [9] just as in the prose accounts of Exodus 14, which, like the Song of the Reed Sea, certainly have no source value in the true sense, but underline what has been said with welcomed clarity.

If, as one can hardly doubt, the destruction of the Egyptians in the sea is originally the essential content of the "original confession of Israel" concerning the leading forth from Egypt,[10] then this very old confession thus praises the Yahweh who saves his people and leads them toward their further history in that he in his war, that is to say Yahweh's war, conquers his and his people's enemies. This is the most conclusive evidence for what has already been said once[11] above concerning the significance of the war of Yahweh. If according to this, provided one may express it in this fashion, there can be no doubt about the superior quality of this confession, so also there can be no doubt as to its quantity when, after the conquest of the land, it "came to be the fundamental religious possession *of all* Israelite tribes." [12] And prior to the conquest of the land? Noth objects to "the readily asked question, which group from the circle of the Israelite tribes that were later united had by chance been the representative of the events in Egypt and at the sea"; "since the

---

[8] See above, p. 13; compare on this problem v. Rad, *Theology*, I, 357.

[9] Compare v. Rad, *Der Heilige Krieg*, pp. 45 ff.

[10] Noth, *Überlieferungsgeschichte*, pp. 52-53; *Contra*, Wellhausen, *Geschichte*, p. 11.

[11] Pp. 41-42.

[12] Noth, *Überlieferungsgeschichte*, p. 53.

subsequently known Israelite tribes established themselves essentially only *with* the conquest of the land in the arable region of Palestine, consequently they had not existed prior to this as tribes." He terms it "moreover improbable that whole tribes had been participating in the questionable events," and assumes "that the clans which had witnessed the events in Egypt and at the sea later incorporated themselves here and there into the alliances of Israelite tribes who were seizing the land and organizing themselves, and indeed into a number of tribes and tribal groups rather than into only one tribe." [13] The latter seems to me improbable, and I am inclined instead to give preference to the old thesis that one must think of the Rachel tribes,[14] even if only—here one has to follow Noth—in the diminished form, that it had scarcely been a question of the whole tribes but rather only of parts of both or of one of the two (Joseph's?) .

To begin with, in my opinion, it need not follow, from our knowing the confession of the leading forth from Egypt only as a common Israelite one, that here, unlike the remainder of the themes of the Pentateuch, "the question as to within which particular tribal group the confession found its conception or at least the peculiar nature of its formation is still irrelevant." [15] We know the other themes also only as common Israelite ones, and Noth nevertheless has managed to demonstrate for each one the relationship to a specific tribal group prior to its expansion into one belonging to Israel as a whole. Among them, the only one that can qualify as common Israelite from the very beginning is the confession of their having been led into the arable land, but even this is valid only in its most general form, failing to make the concrete background visible.[16] Elsewhere—and if we knew the further particulars, perhaps even here—the ques-

---

[13] *Ibid.*

[14] Compare on this point most recently, O. Kaiser, *VT*, 10 (1960) , 1 ff.

[15] Noth, *Überlieferungsgeschichte*, p. 52.

[16] *Ibid.*, p. 55.

tion has to do altogether with the fact that Israel as a whole identified its past with that of one component which was absorbed within it and thus in one way or another adopted from it its special traditions. Even the indisputably exceptional, indeed unique, significance of the "original confession" of the leading forth from Egypt does not justify, at least not *a priori*, the application here of a criterion different from that in the other cases. An originally local tradition is therefore to be assumed here fundamentally as a matter of course.

If, according to the information in Exodus 1:11, one can perceive Ramses II (1290-1223) as the Pharaoh of the oppression[17] and accordingly can place the Exodus from Egypt in the thirteenth century,[18] then the participating groups could have belonged only to the last of the immigrants into Palestine. The Merneptah Stele, which makes mention of an Israel there about 1220, verifies this without concern as to how this verification should be interpreted and especially as to whether the last great immigration thrust there is already presupposed.[19] In view of this, it is difficult not to see in the emigrants from Egypt elements of the Rachel tribes and the first bearers of the tradition of that experience.[20]

Moreover, in my opinion, it now follows as a strong argument that if the presentation of the preceding chapter proves to be correct, the Rachel tribes appear in the arable land as the original and true representatives of the war of Yahweh. One may, indeed one must, trace the line from there back

[17] Doubted by M. A. Beek, *Geschichte Israels* (1961), pp. 23-24.

[18] Noth, *History,* p. 120.

[19] Compare with that Alt, *Kleine Schriften,* I, 163.

[20] G. Hölscher, on the other hand, thinks of the southern tribes (*Geschichtsschreibung in Israel* [1952], pp. 80-81). The proof for this—relationship with Edom; according to Papyrus Anastasi VI, 54 ff., Edomites were admitted into Egypt under Merneptah—is not sufficient, however, for there have probably existed many examples similar to the ones given in those Egyptian notes, and the subsequent proximity of the southern tribes of Israel to Edom does not require a previous common history; the distinct consciousness of the separateness from Edom makes such a case rather unlikely.

to the leading forth from Egypt and therewith term the state of affairs for ancient Israel original to a degree scarcely surpassable. That which at times is completely surprising and solitary, after all, does stand in continuity, and this reaches back to the most venerable event of the past. If the Rachel tribes did lead the wars of Yahweh, or rather let themselves be led in them by their god, then they did so in the footsteps of those who were once led out of Egypt. Even if all Israel could later stand in this continuity, at first only this one segment did so, which itself had come from Egypt and for which the event there was decisive beyond all others.

The origin of the war of Yahweh consequently survives in the tradition about the Mosaic era inasmuch as it belongs from the very beginning to the tribes of middle Palestine. Now this tradition contains not only one but two of the Pentateuchal themes postulated by Noth: in addition to the leading forth from Egypt, also, at least in the case of those who were led forth, the leading into the arable land. I ask myself if, in view of this, one should separate these two themes as sharply as Noth[21] does. That the leading forth is so frequently mentioned apart from the leading in accounts for itself by its importance and alters nothing in the natural progression from the one to the other, which, to be sure, does not make the separation easy.[22] And if the original bearers of the tradition are not in one instance Israel as a whole and in the other, the middle Palestinian tribes, as Noth assumes, but are in both instances the latter, then the separation appears somewhat artificial [23] and an original association appears to be the less complicated and more natural hypothesis. However, this question involving the history of

[21] Überlieferungsgeschichte, pp. 57-58.

[22] Compare W. Zimmerli, Das Alte Testament als Anrede (1956), p. 16; but also Noth, Überlieferungsgeschichte, p. 54.

[23] Perhaps it would be different if one could establish for one segment or the other (not only for individual formulas) distinct places in the cultic life. But for the time being that still does not seem to be the case, despite all the effort spent upon it.

tradition need not occupy us any further in our historical investigation.[24]

Instead, let us put forth another question which is related to the preceding. Within the Pentateuch as a whole, a special position has for some time been attributed to the Sinai pericope literarily, historically, and in the history of tradition.[25] The attempts to rationalize the hiatus to that which precedes and that which follows by means of the assumption of a pilgrimage from Kadesh to Sinai unwittingly contribute more toward increasing the problem than toward eliminating it. Now the question: Does the special position which the Sinai tradition occupies in the Pentateuch perhaps reflect the dualism of Yahweh war and tribal confederation? With due caution Noth has proposed the following combination:[26] the Sinai tradition relates to an event older than the Exodus tradition. Accordingly would "the participants in the encounter with God at Sinai possibly be ranked among the earliest of the segments of the later Israel which appeared in the arable land. . . . In this circle, since Sinai, subjection to the will of God, which was to be formulated in a divine law, would have been decisive, and the significance of the divine law and at the same time that of a central judicature would have had their roots therein. As other elements, who had experienced the deliverance at the 'sea,' were then added in the

[24] It would be favorable to the above view if one did not have to distinguish so sharply between the Pentateuchal theme "leading into the arable land" and the narrative of the conquest of the land in the Book of Joshua, as is done by Noth. The continuity, esp. in the matter of the war of Yahweh, would then be even more evident than it is now. Here v. Rad does not quite yet seem to have given up his opposition to Noth; compare *Theology*, I, 298, n. 4.

[25] Compare Wellhausen, *Composition*, p. 108; *Prolegomena*, pp. 342 ff. (corresponding, by the way, if I understand it correctly, also to the four-source theory by R. Smend, *Die Erzählung des Hexateuch* [1912], pp. 156-57) ; Ed. Meyer, *Die Israeliten und ihre Nachbarstämme* (1906) , pp. 60 ff.; H. Gressmann, *Mose und seine Zeit* (*FRLANT* NF 1 [1913]) , pp. 389 ff.; v. Rad, *Problem*, pp. 13 ff.; Noth, *Überlieferungsgeschichte*, pp. 63 ff.; W. Beyerlin, *Herkunft und Geschichte der ältesten Sinaitradition* (1961). On the other hand, esp. Th. C. Vriezen, *De Godsdienst van Israel* (1963) , pp. 105 ff.

[26] *History*, pp. 134-35.

arable land, the conviction would have immediately im
pressed itself upon them that the mighty God, to whom was
owed the deliverance from Egypt, could have been no other
than the God who appeared at Sinai." Accordingly, the Sinai
tradition contained the foundation of the later amphictyony.
This is clear and in this general form is less vulnerable than
the endeavor to understand Exodus 19 ff. as the legend of a
festival of the formation or of the renewal of the covenant
which would have been celebrated in the amphictyony.[27] If
one asks for which stage of the amphictyony the Sinai tradition has fashioned the etiology, then one may apply Noth's
thesis just referred to thusly: for the six-tribe confederation
of the Leah tribes prior to the expansion into the twelve-tribe
confederation through the admittance of the Rachel tribes.[28]
To be sure this cannot easily be substantiated. Noth infers
his early apposition of the Sinai event from the fact that the
tradition of the leading forth from Egypt now stands "so
much in the foreground of the interest of the Israelite tradition," that one could get the impression "it has, as the fundamental act of God for the existence of Israel, remained in
more recent and direct memory than the appearance of God
at Sinai." [29] But in my opinion one can with at least equal
justification also infer the opposite temporal relation from the
circumstances. That the Sinai tradition for so long a time did
not enter into the total tradition would be explained more
easily by its lateness rather than by its antiquity. It would
then be an etiology created in the time of the twelve-tribe
amphictyony for its existence, its relationship to Yahweh, and
its divine law. The placing of this etiology in the period immediately following the leading forth from Egypt was self-
evident since this was the "canonical" time and was becoming
even more so. Under these circumstances it also is unnecessary to eliminate the figure of Moses from the Sinai tradition,

---

[27] Compare, on the other hand, Noth, *Überlieferungsgeschichte*, pp. 64-65.
[28] Compare Noth, *History*, p. 138, n. 1.
[29] *Ibid.*, p. 134; also *Überlieferungsgeschichte*, p. 65.

which, despite Exodus 24:*1 ff.,[30] can be done only with difficulties. Moses played his role in the Sinai tradition from the very beginning, and he had to do so. That he did not have his original position here, but instead belonged, to begin with, to other complexes of tradition (Noth), remains unaltered by that since in relation to these complexes the Sinai tradition as such is secondary.

I would think that this solution eliminates one further difficulty which is produced by Noth's thesis: according to Noth[31] the name Yahweh "from the beginning was a decisive contribution of the Sinai tradition to the totality of this tradition," and to the elements "who had experienced the deliverance at the 'sea,' the conviction would have immediately impressed itself upon them that the mighty God, to whom was owed the deliverance from Egypt, could have been no other than the God who appeared at Sinai." With that, what is *communis opinio* and—more important—is supported through the testimony of the Song of Miriam, would be denied, namely, the relation of Yahweh to Israel "from the land of Egypt" (Hosea 12:10; 13:4). There are no positive indications that the old six-tribe amphictyony had already worshiped the God Yahweh.[32] According to both, it remains more likely that the Rachel tribes brought with them from the desert the worship of this god whose help they or parts of them had experienced, and then—if one may understand Joshua 24 in this way, under the leadership of Joshua, the first bearer of a name derived from Yahweh known to us[33]—the tribes already settled in the arable land participated in it. And finally the question about the tribal region from which the Sinai tradition would have come

[30] Noth, *Überlieferungsgeschichte*, p. 178.

[31] *History*, p. 138.

[32] If it should have already had the name Israel (Noth, *System*, pp. 83, 91-92), it would be a negative one.

[33] Compare Noth, *Die israelitischen Personennamen* (*BWANT*, Vol. III, no. 10 [1928], p. 107; L. Köhler, *Old Testament Theology* (1957), p. 41, n. 37.

would be superfluous in view of the suggested hypothesis. From the outset, then, what is involved is rather a possession common to all Israel.[34] This does not, of course, exclude the possibility that encounters between Yahweh and people from the circle of Rachel tribes had taken place at Sinai, as indeed it is altogether possible that Sinai was considered to be the seat of Yahweh and as such still remained for a long time the destination of pilgrimages.[35] To be sure, Yahweh comes from here, according to the conception of Deuteronomy 33:2; Judges 5:5; Psalm 68:9, 18 (text emended), passages which do not reveal any influence of the Pentateuch account [36] and from which thus "nothing follows about Sinai as the mountain of *legislation*." [37] "Only a further step managed to make Sinai the scene of the ceremonial disclosure of the special relationship between Yahweh and Israel. It was the poetic necessity that dictated the heightening of the establishing of the people of Yahweh into a dramatic act upon a lofty stage." Even if we are in a position today to say more about the "poetic" than Wellhausen,[38] the essential factor still remains constant. The "further step" belongs in its own way to the series of acts, already referred to repeatedly, in which the war of Yahweh and the tribal confederation grew together. Sinai, from which Yahweh came to the battle of Deborah (he did not come from Shechem!) in order to arouse Israel "from amphictyonic lethargy," [39] as the founding site of the amphictyony, the formation of the covenant there as the continuation of the act of deliverance at the Reed Sea—that

---

[34] Noth thinks of the southern tribes (*Überlieferungsgeschichte*, pp. 66-67) on the one hand because of the late accession to the whole tradition, and on the other, because of the interpolation between elements of the theme "the leading in the wilderness." The first reason can at least hold true just as well for the collective Israelite character; the second, precisely because of the obviously secondary insertion, is in no way conclusive.

[35] Compare I Kings 19 and at that point Noth, *PJB*, 36 (1940), 5 ff.

[36] Compare on this point, Noth, *Überlieferungsgeschichte*, p. 64, n. 186.

[37] Wellhausen, *Composition*, p. 108.

[38] *Geschichte*, p. 12. Compare Beyerlin, *Herkunft und Geschichte der ältesten Sinaitradition*.

[39] Buber, *Königtum*, p. 135.

signifies the projection of the connection of the two poles of Israelite existence before and with Yahweh back into the "classical" past.[40]

In conclusion I wish to say once more emphatically, quoting,[41] "that after all it is merely a question of a conjecture no longer demonstrable, which simply tries to provide an answer to an inevitable question," and that the one who is not "in favor of conjectures" can pass this by. The same holds true for the next chapter.

---

[40] According to the above, to say that in the foreword of the Decalogue Yahweh is represented as the one who has led Israel out of Egypt is not incompatible with the historical separation of the Exodus and Sinai, even when one takes the Decalogue for an original component of the Sinai tradition (compare to that W. Zimmerli, *ThZ*, 16 [1960], 270, n. 8). With that, an objection proposed by J. Bright, *Early Israel in Recent History Writing* (1956), pp. 105-6 and other places, loses weight.

[41] Noth, *History*, p. 138.

7

Moses During the Exodus and at Sinai

At the beginning of Israelite history the figure of Moses stands upon a lonely summit for the tradition. In current historical scholarship it has been somewhat reduced from this elevation. The only way in which scholarship today can approach a figure such as Moses is primarily by a process of subtraction. One proceeds on the basis that the tradition concerning such a figure has grown in the course of time. The important name has, for various reasons, attracted many things to itself which originally had nothing to do with it and has been introduced into areas which were in reality remote from it. This state of affairs is surely the result of the numerous absurdities and anachronisms with which the tradition is burdened. But it also seems to be significant for the more profound insight which is directed toward the structure of the formation of the tradition, and thereby in the "etiological" and "backward projecting" historical reflection discovers elements in which the creative forces of more recent legend-development blend with the memory of the past in this or that period and in this process of blending frequently enough take the lead. In order to get to the beginning, and if possible to the historical nucleus around which the tradition has developed, it is important to exclude everything that is secondary, thus everything which can be explained obviously and naturally by more or less spontaneous acts of modifying (expanding, enlarging, diminishing, making cruder, refining) "etiological" or "backward projecting" legend-development of a later time. The history of scholarly endeavor around the figure of Moses can actually be described for the most part as a history of such subtractions.[1] One can summarize them to the effect that in a number of such operations, which were in many ways interwoven with each other, essentially four kinds of secondary material have been singled out: (1) the "mythical" elements (Eichhorn, Gabler, G. L. Bauer, de Wette); (2) the typical motifs (Gunkel, Gressmann); (3) the law written by the priests (Vatke, Reuss, Kuenen, Wellhausen); (4) entire complexes of narratives (Ed. Meyer, Noth). Concerning the first three points, widespread agreement exists today. The fourth is controversial.

The complex which stands most isolated in the Pentateuch is the series of narratives of the revelation at Sinai. If it is natural on the basis of this isolation, both literary and within the history of tradition, to suspect the historical connection between the Sinai complex and the complexes which surround it, similarly the inference for the figure of Moses is no less obvious. He likely belonged either only to Sinai or only in the remaining material. The second possibility is to be given preference over the first. The most personal of the affairs of Moses which are known—his name, his marriage to a foreigner, his grave—have their place in the tradition elsewhere than at Sinai. That one can only scarcely imagine the Sinai narrative without Moses, as it seems to me, is no effective counter-argument, if one admits that it is more recent than the other Pentateuch themes and from the outset had been composed for the purpose of being inserted in them as an etiology of the tribal confederation of Israel.[2] The picture of Moses as the mediator of the covenant at Sinai, then, shared its secondary character within the total picture of Moses simply with the same situation of the Sinai history within the Pentateuch tradition. That Moses cannot stand at the beginning of the institution of the amphictyony is moreover in-

---

[1] Compare Smend, *Das Mosebild von Heinrich Ewald bis Martin Noth*, pp. 1-21.

[2] Compare above, p. 116.

deed self-evident if one assumes this institution for the first time in the arable land. Rather, if anyone whom we know stands at its beginning, then it is Joshua. That the name of Moses is later claimed for it is understandable. But from where had this name originally received its significance? It is natural to place the "amphictyonic" Moses in relation to one who was a man of the war of Yahweh. His historical place, according to what has been said in the previous chapter, must be sought for at first in connection with the leading forth from Egypt. Noth has denied that Moses belongs there.[3] I believe I am forced to disagree with this denial.

It is difficult to follow Noth in the view that the tradition of the grave of Moses could be the "most original element yet preserved of the tradition of Moses." [4] To be sure there can be no objection to the fact that the statement about the death and burial of Moses in Deuteronomy 34:5-6 in its essential form is older than that which surrounds it.[5] But whether it presupposes "that one was able to point out the grave and revered it as the resting place of a traditional figure," and whether the statement, at the latest Deuteronomic, about the unfamiliarity with the grave site reflects the situation of a later time "in which the site, for reasons unknown to us, was no longer accessible to the Israelites and for that reason its exact location lapsed into oblivion" [6] is difficult to judge. The sole possible alternative to this does not seem to me to be that the "unfamiliarity with the grave of Moses was the original situation and that only subsequently was the grave site of the renowned Moses 'discovered.' " [7]

[3] Particularly *Überlieferungsgeschichte,* pp. 178 ff.
[4] *Ibid.,* pp. 186 ff.
[5] Compare, however, n. 7.
[6] Noth, *Überlieferungsgeschichte,* p. 189.
[7] *Ibid.,* n. 483. I do not know whether one can play the two halves of verse 6 off against each other so strongly as is done by Noth (pp. 188-89). Even the first half does not say much that is precise. That Yahweh in verse 6a had not originally been the subject (p. 188, n. 482) does not seem certain to me. Can "something so extraordinary and shocking" be better formulated than just so briefly and almost "unemphasized and ambiguous" as is here the case? If more were said, would it not seem to be less?

It seems equally conceivable to me that the grave has always been only approximately located in that valley which was known to be situated barely across from the Israelite territory, not because the grave had ever been known, visited, and revered—which the "discovery" would imply—but quite theoretically because the tradition knew Moses in the desert, though not in the arable land, since he was once the leader on the way to the arable land, or had become so, and wanted to let him play his role even to the last possible point. "The narrator wanted to bring him as near as possible to the dwelling place of his people; but he did not even attempt to bring him into Palestine since that conflicted too much with the authentic tradition which knew him only in the desert." [8] That it is a question of "such an obscure site" [9] can be used at least equally well as an argument for this as for the authenticity of the grave tradition. If from this the positive arguments for Noth's thesis do not appear as decisive, there exists nevertheless a compelling counter-argument which has already been expressed on occasion.[10] I quote the words of Bright: if Moses "was only some Transjordanian *sheikh* whose memory was enshrined in a grave tradition—how can it be explained that he so quickly came to be looked upon not only as the leader of all Israel, but positively as its founder?" [11]

An objection of this kind could not be raised against the original relationship of Moses to the tradition of the leading forth from Egypt. F. Schnutenhaus has pointed out [12] that an overlapping of the figure of Moses from the tradition of the

[8] Ed. Meyer, *Die Israeliten und ihre Nachbarstämme* (1906), p. 73.

[9] Noth, *Überlieferungsgeschichte*, pp. 188-89.

[10] E. Osswald, *Das Bild des Mose in der kritischen alttestamentlichen Wissenschaft seit Julius Wellhausen* (Habilitation dissertation, Jena, 1955, typescript), pp. 398-99; J. Bright, *Early Israel in Recent History Writing* (1956), p. 86.

[11] For the criticism on the grave tradition, compare moreover K.-H. Bernhardt, *Gott und Bild*, p. 129, n. 3.

[12] *Die Entstehung der Mosetraditionen* (theological dissertation, Heidelberg, 1958, typescript).

leading forth to the remaining complexes of tradition is easily and naturally conceivable.

The Egyptian name of Moses [13] speaks further for a connection with Egypt. Certainly not everyone who bore an Egyptian name in that time need have been in Egypt;[14] even the Old Testament offers examples of that. But if the tradition affirms of a bearer of an Egyptian name a connection with Egypt, then that is a coincidence which one cannot easily push aside. Also, the assumption that it is "apparently from an extensively Egyptianized section of the people" that Moses originates [15] has a good basis in the name.

However, at present a historical connection with Egypt, be it as probable as can be, is still not identical with the relationship to the Pentateuchal theme of the leading forth from Egypt.[16] Indeed Noth has cited an argument which, if it proves correct, must show this relationship to be secondary. The passage Exodus 5:3 (4) 5-19 sets itself off from its surroundings in "that in it Moses completely withdraws and the Israelite foremen themselves without Moses negotiate with the Pharaoh, while Moses, as it is suddenly and surprisingly revealed in verse 20, has in the meantime waited outside!" Noth sees in this passage "the fossil of a phase in the developing of the tradition in which the figure of Moses had not yet been inserted into the theme 'the leading forth from Egypt,' but rather the elders of the Israelites still func-

---

[13] For the philological aspects, compare J. G. Griffiths, *Journal of Near Eastern Studies* 12 (1953), 225 ff.; on the other hand, M. A. Beek, *Geschichte Israels* (1961), pp. 24-25. The Hebraic meaning as "the one who brought out," which can perhaps be found in Isaiah 63:11 (Beek following Buber, *Moses* [2nd ed., 1952], p. 43), is in this context of no great value. In Exodus 2:10 it cannot be found precisely so, and that it is there by "secret design" (Buber, *Moses*) seems to me to be out of the question.

[14] Noth, *Überlieferungsgeschichte*, pp. 178-79. Compare, however, since then Noth, *History*, p. 136, n. 2.

[15] Buber, *Moses*.

[16] G. Hölscher considers it possible that Moses was Egyptian, but denies his participation in the Exodus (*Geschichtsschreibung in Israel* [1952], pp. 82-83).

tioned as spokesmen over against the Egyptians." [17] The state of affairs in Exodus 5 seems to me to be indisputable, but not the explanation. The fact that Moses does not appear in this passage does not have to mean that originally he did not at all belong to the leading forth from Egypt. On the contrary, to begin with, one can regard it as quite appropriate that in those situations in which it is a question of the aggravation of compulsory labor and the measure to be affected by it, the (Egyptian) "taskmasters" (נגשים) and the (Israelite) "overseers" (שטרים) [18] are for the Pharaoh the partners that exist in order to receive his instructions or else to complain to him, even if the initiative for the entire incident came from the other party. As a result it is significant when Moses in this phase remains in the background. By all means, then, even the disappearance of Moses (and of Aaron) at the beginning of our passage and still more the manner of reappearance in verse 20 do seem to be strange and strongly favor Noth's supposition of a special position of our passage, even if not an implicitly literary one. Verse 1, 2 (4), and 20 ff. apparently do not originally belong together with it. Does it consequently exclude the role of Moses? I do not believe so, and for the explanation of the peculiar situation in Chapter 5, I would like to refer to a phenomenon which occurs in a completely different connection, namely in I Kings 12. The situation has features similar to that in Exodus 5. The people of Israel beg the king (or rather the one who is to become king) Rehoboam for an easing of the burdens which lie upon them. The king reacts negatively, whereupon the people rebel against him. Instead of Rehoboam, they make Jeroboam their king. According to the original text, which is still preserved in the Septuagint, he had not participated in the negotiations with Rehoboam. Rather he had stayed in Egypt, whence he had once fled from Solomon, and returned upon

---

[17] *Überlieferungsgeschichte*, p. 76; compare also Noth in the *Exoduskommentar* at this point.

[18] "Elders" are out of the question!

the news of his death (verse 2, text emended). Israel learns of that after the failure of the negotiations with Rehoboam, sends for him, has him called into the meeting, and makes him king (verse 20). According to the precepts of the narrative art, this course of events is the proper one. A figure destined to help in an emergency (and Jeroboam may also be considered as such) tends to put in an appearance only when it is necessary. Before that he exists only in secret, known to the listener or reader as already appointed [19] and possibly even through an initial deed in a smaller scope[20] as already proved. The moment of suspense consists of when and how the general emergency makes it necessary for the hero to come forth[21] from his seclusion[22] and meet the emergency. It can be verified a hundredfold that this moment is delayed as long as possible. A deliverer seldom comes too early. But on the other hand, there are also invariably listeners, readers, and narrators who cannot wait for it, because they fail to recognize the moment of suspense or cannot imagine even the preliminary actions without the participation of the hero who is secretly already present, even if only in the background, and who controls the scene. Such persons have subsequently had Jeroboam participate in the negotiations of the people with Rehoboam (I Kings 12:3, 12 MT). I suspect the same process in Exodus 5, even if it is no longer perceptible there on the basis of textual criticism (which is, of course, anyhow an extraordinary stroke of luck). Moses, in fact, does not belong in the negotiations there, not because he does not have anything to do originally with the leading forth from Egypt, but because his public appearance already presupposes the ineffectual development of the negotiations. The beginning of the chapter is accordingly the counterpart

---

[19] Jeroboam: I Kings 11:29 ff.; Moses: Exodus 3-4.

[20] Jeroboam: I Kings 11:26-28 (one expects between verse 28 and verse 40 something other than the account of the call); Moses: Exodus 2:11 ff.

[21] Return from the exile in the case of Jeroboam: I Kings 12:2; by Moses: Exodus 4:20.

[22] Jeroboam: I Kings 11:40; Moses: Exodus 2:15.

to the Masoretic supplements in I Kings 12:3, 12. The insertion of Moses following verse 19 is not—here the situation differs from that of Jeroboam—preserved for us; the present verses 20 ff. belong to the same literary stratum, or at least to the development of the same tradition, as the beginning of the chapter. What they could have replaced can, at the most, be conjectured.[23] The question can scarcely be answered, therefore, because it is uncertain whether Exodus 5:*3-19 is already aiming toward the account of the plagues [24] or rather whether it did not belong to an older phase of the formation of the tradition in which the account of the plagues,[25] which grew out of the rite of the Passover, did not yet belong to the theme of the leading forth from Egypt. I would not know what should be said against the second possibility, that is, against the fact that Exodus 5:*3-19 would be older in the history of the tradition than the account of the plagues and beyond this—possibly by imagining an insertion no longer preserved of Moses as leader of the people —that it should be combined with the tradition of the leading forth itself, if one indeed wishes to obtain, certainly not the oldest but perhaps an older form of the narrative formation of the Exodus tradition than is presently available to us. Be that as it may, the sequence of narratives can be understood as the history, or better, the series of stories of the charismatic hero Moses, whose person is quite inextricably interwoven into the Exodus tradition, whereon—if there is some truth to the furnished explanation—his absence in Exodus 5:*3-19 cannot be confusing. This series of stories begins at present with the birth legend in Exodus 2:1-10, or already with what precedes it in Chapter 1 as an exposition, and ends with the act of liberation at the sea. The evidence

[23] Was it perhaps the account of the call which now seems to break the connection between 2:23aα and 4:19, 20a? Compare Noth, *Überlieferungsgeschichte*, p. 31, n. 103.

[24] Thus Noth, *Überlieferungsgeschichte*, p. 76.

[25] Compare *ibid.*, pp. 70 ff.

that Moses is here being conceived of and represented as a charismatic leader could easily be augmented beyond what was brought forth in the Jeroboam account. Alt in the last years of his life expressed repeatedly in his lectures the suspicion that the historical Moses has to be understood according to the analogy of the later charismatic leaders of Israel.[26] This has a basis in Exodus 1-14 to the extent that even here Moses apparently is already understood in this way and not as priest, prophet, or such kind.[27]

The historicity of Moses in the role of the first of the "major Judges" of course cannot be proved—but also it cannot be disproved, and the Egyptian name and the ease with which Moses from here on could grow into his future roles,[28] whether historically or only in the developing of the tradition, may certainly be taken as positive clues. Can more yet be said? I would like to draw attention to the possibility of a connection between Moses and the symbol of the war of Yahweh, the Ark. Wellhausen was once of the opinion[29] that this has "for itself the presumption of being the most historical of what we know about him (Moses)." The proposition cannot be repeated so apodictically. But it need not be entirely false. That the Pentateuch contains nothing reliable concerning the Ark in the period in the wilderness, in particular no report about its preparation,[30] is not a very

[26] Compare Smend, *Das Mosebild von Heinrich Ewald bis Martin Noth*, pp. 59-60.

[27] A certain similarity to the prophet is of course, conceded particularly in the Yahwist version of the account of the call; compare Noth, *Exodus* (1962), pp. 40-41. The distance from the charismatic leader there is also basically not great.

[28] That later he no longer appears as a charismatic leader does not say anything against this as his first role. This has its place, as far as we can determine, only in the case of the leading forth from Egypt. Exodus 17:8 ff., where it is a question of a war of Yahweh but where Moses does not appear as a charismatic leader in the manner perhaps to be expected, is in no way a counter-argument apart from the fact that Moses could have been inserted here only later (compare Noth, *Überlieferungsgeschichte*, pp. 182-83).

[29] *Geschichte*, p. 27.

[30] It has often been suspected that such a report once stood between Exodus 33:6 and 7 and was struck out with regard to the parallel account of the priestly writing; compare Wellhausen, *Composition*, p. 93, and many

grave deficiency. Reliable accounts are simply not to be expected in the Pentateuch, and it would be rather surprising if they were there. One must restrict himself to the conditions in later and better documented periods. Can the origin of the Ark in the arable land be proved on the basis of these? To that end some have preferred to utilize the cows which, according to I Samuel 6:7, 10, 12, 13, were harnessed to the Ark.[31] But there it is a question of a highly unusual case.[32] One refers further to the competition with the cloud as the symbol of leadership.[33] But we do not know if only one such tradition could exist; moreover, the cloud no doubt belongs together with Sinai, something which in the case of the Ark, if it has anything to do with Moses and thus with the Exodus from Egypt, is improbable.[34] The chief argument tends to be the names of the Ark in I Samuel 4-6 and II Samuel 6 where ארון האלהים has predominance over ארון יהוה, thus a situation could be dimly visible in which the Ark did not yet belong to Yahweh. However that is not very certain. If for the narrators a slight doubt had existed with regard to the proprietor of the Ark, it would have been easy for them to insert יהוה for האלהים, not only primarily there when the Ark is persent in the land of the Philistines,[35] but also otherwise. Just the indiscriminateness, in my opinion, warns against looking behind the names for too much that is fundamental and wanting to find in them a basis for historical processes which at the time of the narrative already lay in the distant past. The same is true for the expression שם שם יהוה צבאות ישב הכרבים עליו. ארון האלהים אשר־נקרא (II Sam-

others down to v. Rad, *Theology*, I, 237, n. 109; on the other hand, most recently, Noth, on this passage and *Überlieferungsgeschichte*, p. 224.

[31] Perchance R. Hartmann, *ZAW*, 37 (1917/18), 236.

[32] *Contra*, J. Dus, *ThZ*, 17 (1961), 3-4.

[33] B. Stade, *Theologie des Alten Testaments*, I (1905), 44; v. Rad, *Problem*, pp. 117-18.

[34] If anything, Noth is inclined to view the Ark in the Sinai tradition (*Überlieferungsgeschichte*, pp. 224-25), but on the basis of his hypothesis, contested above, of the identity of the Ark with the amphictyonic central sanctuary.

[35] v. Rad, *Problem*, p. 115.

uel 6:2) in which some like to find the takeover of an originally Canaanite object of worship by the God Yahweh stated
expressis verbis.[36] In addition, as I. L. Seeligmann points out
with new arguments,[37] one must at this point, according to
Ehrlich, read the first שם probably as *shām* and strike out all
that follows (compare I Chronicles 13:6) and understand
נקרא according to II Samuel 1:6; 18:9; 20:1 whereby the passage completely fails to sustain the thesis referred to.

That it stands in Shiloh in the area of the Rachel tribes
speaks in behalf of an origin of the Ark in the desert—but
this is not compelling, of course, since it could have already
been in Shiloh previously and was thereupon adopted by the
immigrants.[38] Equally limited is the value of the analogy
of Bedouin sanctuaries which has often been referred to.[39]
Should Galling be correct in that one could conclude from
I Kings 12:28 that as far as the leading forth from Egypt [40] is
concerned, the Ark-sanctuary was especially thought of, that
would also not be a matter of indifference for our context;
yet this interpretation of the words of Jeroboam is not so
compelling that one may rely upon them too much. The
names and descendants of the sons of Eli in Shiloh seem more
important to me. I Samuel 2:27 is certainly no useful evidence; the reference to Moses rather than to Aaron or Levi [41]
is not likely, and considering the very recent origin of the
passage would also be of no great historical value. But the
names Hophni and Phinehas are Egyptian, as is the name
Moses. Since Egyptian names in Israel are as a rule very

[36] Compare M. Dibelius, *Die Lade Jahwes,* pp. 20 ff.; v. Rad, *Problem,*
p. 116; above all, K. Galling, *ThLZ,* Vol. 81 (1956), columns 68-69; E. Kutsch,
RGG[3] IV (1960), column 198.

[37] *VT,* 11 (1961), 204-5.

[38] Thus, for example, M. Dibelius, *Die Lade Jahwes,* pp. 118-19.

[39] Rightly skeptical is E. Kutsch, *RGG*[3] IV, column 198.

[40] K. Galling, *Die Erwählungstraditionen Israels (BZAW,* 48 [1928]), 74.

[41] Wellhausen, *Prolegomena,* p. 142; Stade, *Theologie des Alten Testaments,* I, 43; R. Smend, *Alttestamentliche Religionsgeschichte* (2nd ed.,
1899), p. 72; *Die Erzählung des Hexateuch* (1912), p. 354.

rare,[42] a connection is by no means to be excluded. Some have wanted to identify this still more precisely. The name Phinehas is also borne by an older Israelite, repeatedly mentioned as a priest after whom a place in Ephraim is named (Joshua 24:33). This Phinehas who is called into question [43] is considered to be the son of Eleazar, the son of Aaron (Exodus 6:25; Joshua 22:13, 30 ff.; Judges 20:28, and in other instances). By substituting Eliezer, the son of Moses (Exodus 18:4), for Eleazar, the son of Aaron, a lineage of Moses has been postulated as being more original, in agreement with the fact that the lineage of Aaron in later time was characteristic of the true priesthood.[44] This is, of course, an undemonstrable conjecture.[45] It is, however, independent of the observation of the Egyptian character of the names of the sons of Eli and of Moses (and indeed already expressed earlier), and precisely in their mutual independence both may gain in importance. Moreover, neither the one nor the other is dependent upon the fact that the Ark originated in the wilderness and that Moses had already been connected with it. If this cult object had only been adopted by the immigrating Josephites in Shiloh, then its care was simply taken over by the Mosaic line which linked it firmly with the tradition of the war of Yahweh which was brought along. The warlike character of the Ark would also in this case be an argument for the role of Moses postulated above.

What has been said concerning Moses in the foregoing is undemonstrable; that cannot be helped. Moreover it is in-

[42] Compare M. Noth, *Die israelitischen Personennamen* (*BWANT*, Vol. III, no. 40 [1928]), p. 23. The general assignment there to Levi is contestable.
[43] Compare also Noth on Joshua 24:33.
[44] Wellhausen, *Prolegomena*, pp. 142-43; Ed. Meyer, *Die Israeliten und ihre Nachbarstämme* (1906), pp. 92-93, 450; Smend, *Die Erzählung des Hexateuch*, pp. 352 ff.; Gressmann, *Mose und seine Zeit*, pp. 274-75; E. Auerbach, *Wüste und gelobtes Land*, I (1932), 98-99; O. Eissfeldt, *ZAW*, 58 (1940/41), 198.
[45] From the position of Exodus 18:4 after Exodus 2:22 (and 18:3) one can conclude that the group of Eliezers were not derived from Moses very early (Noth, *Überlieferungsgeschichte*, p. 203).

sufficient; something can be done about that, even if it is not much. Of the most personal elements which are known to us about Moses, one has not yet appeared: the marriage to a foreign wife. It will be quite evident that she has to be at least as important a reference point as the name and the grave. The threefold testimony speaks clearly for the fact that it is a question of a historical element.[46] But one difficulty stands in the way of an evaluation. If one grants the presupposition of Noth, that Moses originally belonged in only one of the Pentateuchal themes,[47] then there appears to be no more room for the marriage to the foreigner. She seems to belong to the theme "leading in the desert." [48] But above, Moses was claimed for the leading forth from Egypt. Must this now be corrected? I do not believe so. To the history of the charismatic Moses belongs the motif of his flight and return.[49] With this motif the Pentateuchal theme of the leading forth from Egypt is not abandoned, even if the locality does temporarily change. The local digression in this instance is thus not an indication of the original independence of the two traditions,[50] but rather lies in the logic of only one. But thereupon the narrative of the visit of Moses' father-in-law to the mountain of God (Exodus 18), which according to Noth[51] stands "in many respects peculiarly isolated" and therefore belongs to the theme "the leading in the wilderness" strictly speaking only because it takes place

[46] Noth, *Überlieferungsgeschichte*, p. 185.

[47] I would not necessarily share this assumption for Noth's themes "leading forth from Egypt" and "leading into the arable land"; compare on this point p. 114 above. The relationship to the first would not exclude that to the latter.

[48] Noth, *Überlieferungsgeschichte*, pp. 184-85.

[49] See above, p. 126.

[50] Moreover, a local "point of contact" in the sense that narratives are being passed on at the site at which they take place or about which they should otherwise testify to something else, can hardly be meant here, at least as far as the Exodus tradition is concerned. Persisting in the separation of the traditions is A. H. J. Gunneweg, *ZThK*, 61 (1964), 1 ff., who moreover in this context affirms "an altogether too hasty leap from the history of tradition into history" (p. 3, n. 8).

[51] *Überlieferungsgeschichte*, pp. 150-51.

in the wilderness and "has not the least to do in the history of tradition" with the Sinai theme, moves into proximity with the Exodus tradition. Indeed, the bare motif of flight and return could, if need be, be sufficient within the context of the narrative of the charismatic Moses. But only if absolutely necessary. Possibly the encounter with God could be imagined as absent, although in the present context it is indeed what actually sets the Exodus event in motion. However, the most compelling statements about the circumstances at the place of refuge are hardly dispensable: the Midianites and Moses' relationship to them through marriage. But thereupon Exodus 18 is acknowledged as a continuation, indeed it is required.[52] That one therewith goes beyond the leading forth from Egypt is not necessarily a counter-argument; the context of an old narrative does not need to confrom exactly to that which appears to us today as a "theme." [53] If there is some truth in all that has been said, then it is not ruled out as far as the history of the tradition is concerned that Moses at the same time was the leader in the Exodus from Egypt and stood in a close personal relationship with the Midianites, a relationship which led [54] to the cultic association between Midianite and "Israelite" elements (Exodus 18 in the first half of the traditional material to be found there) .[55] It is difficult in view of this to reject the so-called Midianite or Kenite hypothesis, according to which Yahweh was originally the god of the Midianites or

[52] It makes no difference that Exodus 18 is Elohistic, again the flight narrative is Yahwistic; compare Noth, *Überlieferungsgeschichte*, p. 222, n. 551.

[53] One difficulty lies in the fact that the Exodus tradition is above attributed to the Rachel tribes, whereas the tradition of the mountain of God is being attributed to the southern tribes by Noth, *Überlieferungsgeschichte*, p. 152. The main argument, however, in the case of Noth is the very loose relationship to the theme "leading in the wilderness." Even the reference to I Kings 19:3 (compare Noth, *Überlieferungsgeschichte*, notes 393-94) is not decisive, for it is obvious that in later time pilgrimages to the mountain of God led through the territory of the southern tribes.

[54] Or did it already depend upon this association?

[55] Noth, *Überlieferungsgeschichte*, p. 150.

Kenites and through Moses became the god of those who had been led out of Egypt.[56]

This is not the place to discuss further the problem of Moses. Nevertheless, what has already been said seems to leave open the possibility that at the beginning of the relationship between Yahweh and "Israel" actually stood the person of Moses; further, that this relationship found its first great expression in an act of war of the god. The war of Yahweh, according to that, would have actually been the original element of what in time was destined to become the religion of Israel.[57] To this original element the amphictyonic element was later added as a second, or rather not as a second but as a third or fourth. Hence one does not, with Sellin[58] have to affirm and deplore a subsequent politicizing of the religion of Yahweh. The political—or, as Buber says,[59] the theopolitical—on the contrary already stands at the beginning and is personified in the figure of Moses. The amphictyony is of a different type, an organization in which the theopolitical element is not included from the beginning and which only after many generations has to be gradually conquered by that element which at first survived outside

---

[56] The arguments for it do not need to be enumerated here; compare esp. H. H. Rowley, *From Joseph to Joshua* (1950), pp. 153 ff.; *ZAW*, 69 (1957), 10 ff. and the literature referred to therein; K.-H. Bernhardt, *Gott und Bild*, pp. 125 ff.; v. Rad, *Theology*, I, 9. Naturally enough, difficulties remain. Not the least of these consists of the vacillation in the tradition between the Midianite and Kenite (Judges 1:16; 4:11) origin of the father-in-law of Moses (add to that, though probably not of equal importance, Numbers 12:1). The usual harmonization, according to which the Kenites in those days had been a sub-group of the Midianites, is not quite satisfying; but in view of the geographical fluctuation of the Kenites which is to be observed in the Old Testament, it can be quite correct.

[57] The action of Jael (Judges 4:17 ff.; 5:24 ff.), the Kenite who achieved the victory in the war of Yahweh, could also speak in behalf of the claim of the connecting line drawn above from the Exodus from Egypt to the encounter at the mountain of God or from the first war of Yahweh to the Midianites or Kenites. That a member of the supposed original circle of devotees of the god steps forward precisely here is nevertheless noteworthy. Unfortunately the text does not yield any additional clues.

[58] *Geschichte des israelitisch-jüdischen Volkes*, I (1924), 102.

[59] Compare on the following, Buber, *Königtum*, pp. 128 ff.

the amphictyony in the wars of Yahweh. For that reason to set the amphictyony over against the Mosaic "Israel" as a complete contrast, to hold the theopolitical Moses up to a "non-political-sacred" Joshua is of course hardly equitable. For if the Josephite Joshua should have actually founded the twelve-tribe confederation, then this was not merely an act of renunciation and adaptation. In this act Yahweh, the god of the last immigrants, became the god of all twelve tribes and remained so. The decisive expressions of the relationship between Yahweh and Israel may have been the wars, which were led neither by the amphictyonic institution nor by all the tribes—apart from the institution, the principle "Yahweh the God of Israel, Israel the people of Yahweh" would perhaps never have existed. Beyond that, still more Mosaic material may have found its way into the institution, for instance, into its divine law.[60] We do not know that, because we know far too little not only about the amphictyony but also about Moses.

---

[60] Is the peculiarly isolated sentence in Exodus 15:25b perhaps a basis for this?

Abbreviations

AThANT	=	Abhandlungen zur Theologie des Alten und Neuen Testaments
BBB	=	Bonner biblische Beiträge
BFchrTh	=	Beiträge zur Förderung christlicher Theologie
BWA(N)T	=	Beiträge zur Wissenschaft vom Alten (und Neuen) Testament
BZ	=	Biblische Zeitschrift
BZAW	=	Beihefte zur Zeitschrift für die alttestamentliche Wissenschaft
FRLANT	=	Forschungen zur Religion und Literatur des Alten und Neuen Testaments
JBL	=	Journal of Biblical Literature
IEJ	=	Israel Exploration Journal
PJB	=	Palästinejahrbuch
PRE	=	Realencyklopädie für protestantische Theologie und Kirche
RB	=	Révue biblique
RE	=	Realencyklopädie der classischen Altertumswissenschaft, Neue Bearbeitung
RGG	=	Die Religion in Geschichte und Gegenwart
ThLZ	=	Theologische Literaturzeitung
ThStKr	=	Theologische Studien und Kritiken
ThZ	=	Theologische Zeitschrift
VT	=	Vetus Testamentum
ZAW	=	Zeitschrift für die alttestamentliche Wissenschaft
ZDPV	=	Zietschrift des Deutschen Palästinavereins
ZWTh	=	Zeitschrift für wissenschaftliche Theologie

Abbreviations of Works Frequently Cited

A. Alt,	Essays=Essays on Old Testament History and Religion (1966)
——,	Kleine Schriften=Kleine Schriften zur Geschichte des Volkes Israel, I, II (2nd ed., 1959), III (1959)
M. Buber,	Königtum=Königtum Gottes (3rd ed., 1956)
M. Noth,	History=The History of Israel (2nd ed., 1960)
——,	Laws=The Laws in the Pentateuch and Other Studies (1966)
——,	System=Das System der zwölf Stämme Israels (BWANT, Vol. IV, no. 1 [1930])
——,	Überlieferungsgeschichte=Überlieferungsgeschichte des Pentateuch (2nd ed., 1960)
——,	Überlieferungsgeschichtliche Studien=Überlieferungsgeschichtliche Studien (2nd ed., 1957)
G. v. Rad,	Der Heilige Krieg=Der Heilige Krieg im alten Israel (2nd ed., 1952)
——,	Problem=The Problem of the Hexateuch and Other Essays (1966)
——,	Old Testament Theology, I (1962), II (1965)

137

J. Wellhausen,   Composition=Die Composition des Hexa-
                 teuchs und der historischen Bücher des
                 Alten Testaments (3rd ed., 1899)

————,   Geschichte=Israelitische und jüdische Ges-
                 chichte (7th ed., 1914)

————,   Prolegomena=Prolegomena to the History
                 of Ancient Israel (1957)

Index of Authors

139

Index of Passages